DEEPERWOMEN™

TEACH

Stories and Strategies for Life, Love, and Leaderhip from Women Who Lead

A Literary Collaborative By

Dr. Barbara Swinney

Featuring Expert Authors

Dr. Leona Allen
Pamela Dingle
Jeri Godhigh
Lorarine Loving
Jamia Ponder
Dr. Marcea Whitaker
Nile Yates

DEEPER Women™ Teach

PUBLISHING COMPANY

P.O. Box 3401
Atlanta, Georgia

Copyright © 2021 by Dr. Barbara Swinney

Cover Design:
BSI Publishing Company

Book Design:
BSI Publishing Company
www.bsipublishing.com

Books by BSI Publishing Company may be purchased for educational, business, or promotional use. For information, please email info@bsipublishing.com

Permission granted to use stories by individuals included for demonstration.

All rights reserved. Except as permitted under the U.S. Copyright Act of 1976, no part of this publication may be reproduced, distributed, or transmitted in any form or by any means, or in a database or retrieval system, without the prior written permission of the publisher.

First printing: April 2021

All right reserved.

978-1-7325253-2-0

Printed in the United States of America

DEDICATION

To every woman who leads—

navigating the demands of her role as life happens

right in the middle of her leadership.

About the Brand

DEEPER Women™ Speak..DEEPER Women™ Lead… DEEPER Women™ Teach!

The DEEPER Women™ Brand was created in 2018 with the launch of Dr. Barbara Swinney's first book, "It's Always DEEPER: Six Steps to Achieving Perpetual Success"—the feature at the first DEEPER Women™ Conference, DEEPER Women™ Speak. This conference would establish the brand as a platform for women who lead to share their stories and strategies for life, love, and leadership. It would be the first in a series of DEEPER Women™ events and products. Since the launch (the brand, in collaboration with BSI Life and Leadership Consulting and BSI Publishing) has expanded to include the establishment of The DEEPER Leader Institute for Personal and Professional Development (an accredited coaching certification institute), the "Living the DEEPER Life" Companion Journal, the DEEPER Women™ Lead Annual Conference; and now, this

DEEPER Women™ Teach

Literary Collaborative-"DEEPER Women™ Teach: Stories and strategies for life, love, and leadership from women who lead."

DEEPER Women™ Teach

Tenets of a **DEEPER** Woman™

What exactly is a DEEPER Woman™? There are certain characteristics that a DEEPER Woman demonstrates. These powerful women, the authors of this book, all exemplify what it truly means to be a DEEPER Woman™. They all have and continue to healthily navigate the turbulence of life, love, and leadership while balancing the demands in their roles as leaders. They are proven by circumstances, experiences, training, and trade. They are indeed DEEPER Women™.

The **DEEPER** Woman™—

- knows who she is and understands that her purpose is far greater than she is.
- is not intimidated by another woman's gifts. In fact, she understands that it is her job to help identify and cultivate those gifts.

DEEPER Women™ Teach

- does not shake in the face of her problems. She understands that her problems come only as a means to establish her as someone else's solution.
- understands that her only function is to be the light. When you are the light, you cannot complain about the darkness. All you can do is shine!
- is no longer afraid to face herself, nor does she quake at what others think of her. She is confident, sure in her purpose, and has learned to live The DEEPER Life!

DEEPER is not just a hashtag, tagline, or a book. DEEPER is a lifestyle!

Table of Contents

Preface   10

Want Your Life to Go Higher? Go DEEPER!   13
    -Dr. Barbara Swinney

From Struggle Comes Strength   43
    -Dr. Leona Allen

Broken to be Blessed   63
    -Pamela Dingle

Who is Sleeping with Your Husband?   85
    -Jeri Godhigh

Hold On and Fight   97
    -Lorarine Loving

More Than The Mrs.   109
    -Jamia Ponder

Who Are You?   125
    -Dr. Marcea Whitaker

Nobody Knew the Journey   138
    -Nile Yates

Meet the Authors   151

Preface

My name is Dr. Barbara Swinney...and I am Iyanla Vanzant; I am Michelle Obama; I am Oprah Winfrey; I am Yolanda, Becky, and Lisa...I am You!

When I started this journey of healing and leading, I kept bumping into myself; I kept running into Barbara, but I did not recognize her because she looked like you. I heard untold story after untold story; stories that could have unlocked my alabaster box twenty years ago—but nobody could step outside of themselves long enough to free me. I heard stories of toxic relationships, of mental, emotional, and spiritual suppression, of illnesses caused by the stress of abuse, and the tragic outcomes of cyclical dysfunction.

Sadly, most of the women I spoke with were telling their stories for the first time...to me! They had spent years of going it alone, years of hopelessness and silent frustration. They had done the same thing I was guilty of doing—putting on my Red Ruby Woo Lipstick and heels and walking around confidently insecure, bound by the expectations of others, paralyzed by self-judgment, and completely afraid to give any indication that I was not OK.

That is why I became vigilant about helping women, like you, transition through life-changing events, while managing the demands of their roles as leaders. That is why this book is so important. DEEPER Women™ are real women, tackling real issues, leading in the real world, and living a real life.

This literary collaborative, written by eight powerful DEEPER Women™ who lead, is a collection of stories and strategies for life, love, and leadership to empower other women who lead! Get to know the authors through their stories and learn about how they experienced breakthrough and breakout; learn how you can heal and lead in your profession. To get the most out of this book, take notes and be intentional in implementing the tips and strategies provided to

DEEPER Women™ Teach

help you navigate life as it happens right in the middle of your leadership.

Want Your Life to Go Higher?
Go DEEPER!

By Dr. Barbara Swinney

DEEPER Women™ Teach

Everything I thought I would say, I did not. I anxiously waited to meet with my counselor to discuss the demise of my marriage. I had my tears on ready and my anger set to trigger; just waiting to let her eavesdrop on the conversation in my head; the inner banter about how I found out that my husband was living a double life for years and within thirty days of our divorce, he was engaged. How was I supposed to help my girls navigate this dysfunction? How was I going to hide my grief from the people at work; the people I was charged to lead? The humiliation of it all—the pain and agony of realizing that the last twenty years of my life was an illusion, of sorts, was bewildering. The man that my girls and I greeted at the door upon his return from his "business trips", was really returning to us from his other life—one in which we did not exist. In this house of cards, she was the "wife". Who does this? The depth of the deception was overwhelming and left me questioning my identity, my judgement...my intelligence. Reassuring myself, I continued to engage, "I know I'm smart; brilliant in fact". "I'm a good woman. Any man would love to have me love him. How did I miss this? Why did I allow myself to accept so little?"

The counselor entered the office. We exchanged pleasantries and then it was time, time for me to let her in on my diatribe! I opened my mouth, ready to spew it all and...NOTHING! None of the thoughts would form into words. In the very moment that I attempted to speak, I had a stunning revelation. Almost every sentence or question I posed during my mental babbling included the word "I" (How did "I" miss this?; "I" allowed...; "I" lost...). It became clear that "I" was in the middle of it all. The anger and urge to blame dissipated. I became less interested in hating my ex and more concerned about my own healing. If I were going to *live* a full life for the rest of my life, I would have to take the steps necessary to mend my broken heart.

DEEPER Women™ Teach

I knew that if I wanted my life to go higher, I would have to go D-E-E-P-E-R!

This is exactly where the DEEPER Framework was established. While writing my first book, "It's Always DEEPER", I developed the framework to help readers get unstuck. As I began to heal, I found myself using the concept to help me navigate the healing process. I have included the framework here for your reference as you continue to heal and lead on your journey to you.

D*iscover Your Purpose and* ***D****ecide What You Want—*

>Clarify your vision and get clear about what you would like to accomplish.

***E**xamine Your Life—*

>Identify behaviors that have impeded your progress. Figure out why you do what you do.

DEEPER Women™ Teach

Eliminate the Barriers—

> Replace negative behaviors with those that move you toward your goals and the life you want to live.

Plan of Action—

> Determine the steps necessary to get what you want! Be specific and intentional in the action steps to accomplish your goals.

Evaluate Your Progress—

> Get honest with yourself regarding your progress. Celebrate and make adjustments as necessary.

Realize That You Can Do It!—

> Apply these principles in life and you WILL reach your goals and become who you want to be!

DEEPER Women™ Teach

Discover Your Purpose and Decide What You Want—

At the same time that I learned of long-term infidelity in my marriage, I also experienced a significant shift in my career as a leader in education. Twenty years in a career—with nothing less than exemplary ratings, —I was literally, tapped on the shoulder and told that my services were no longer needed in the position. Without explanation, I was technically demoted…in my marriage and in my career. The two things with which I most readily identified were stripped away. This compounded the devastation. Who was I without them?

Somewhere on life's path, I had lost my way. My identity had become enmeshed with that of my marriage and my career, I simply lost track of Barbara. I had to get clear about who I was, who I wanted to become, and what I wanted. It was important to establish a new vision for myself. I started with ***deciding*** to take 100% responsibility for my life.

DEEPER Women™ Teach

Nothing that happened to me was my fault, but it was certainly my responsibility. It was I, who accepted less than I deserved (at home and at work), who ignored signs of emotional abandonment and infidelity, who did not hold my former partner accountable, over depended on my career for validation, and stayed in both relationships much longer than morally obligated. My behavior was not aligned with what I had envisioned for my life, but I made no adjustments (other than hope and pray that he would change and that I would regain a similar leadership position).

I did not honor myself. I gave too much power to other people, career status, things, and ideals. The onus was on me to fix this. **Deciding** to accept responsibility for my part in the demise of my marriage and the unraveling of my career, I was able to determine a path forward.

Getting a different result in my life started with *deciding* that I wanted something different…to become

DEEPER Women™ Teach

something different—a return to and unfolding of who I have always been.

Go DEEPER:

At times, we all get stuck (in relationships, careers, or even in our own beliefs)—feeling like our life just is not what we envisioned it to be. You give your all to other people, entities, or ideals; the "real" you silenced by the noise that life creates. If you have lost your way or become a little foggy about who you are and what you really want, DECIDING that you want something different is a great place to start. Take the time to contemplate the questions below. Use the DEEPER Thinking Spaces to process your responses:

Who am I?

_____

_____

_____

_____

_____

_____

DEEPER Women™ Teach

Where am I from? (understanding your absolute origin will bring clarity of identity and purpose)

_____

_____

_____

_____

_____

_____

_____

What is it that I really want?

_____

_____

_____

_____

_____

_____

_____

DEEPER Women™ Teach

What are my gifts? How am I using my gifts to serve others?

_____

_____

_____

_____

_____

_____

_____

Examine Your Life—

This was probably the most difficult process of all. I really had to figure out why I was doing what I was doing; *examine* behaviors that had me stuck in a relationship and a career. I had to ask myself, "Why?...Why haven't I taken the actions necessary to acquire what I want; to live the life that I truly wanted to live, or to become who I had hoped to be?"

When I actually took the time to consider these questions, I discovered purpose in the pain of the divorce and demotion.

As I started to examine my marriage, I found dependent behavior that started long before the marriage. I was so concerned about what people, including my former husband, colleagues, and those under my leadership, thought of me. All of my life of pursuing something—a degree, a promotion, status, the big house with the wrought iron fence, the husband, two kids, and the dog! The perfect "looking" life. What was the root of this need to please or being perceived as the perfect package? What was at the bottom of all of this?

Growing up, the youngest of ten, was like having my own little entourage to support and cheer me on from the very beginning. I remember times when my brothers and sisters would literally have physical fights over taking me, THE BABY, on a trip to a friend's house or showing me off to that special someone. My family openly celebrated my every milestone and constantly sent the "Midas Touch" message to me. When I started walking, they erupted with praises, "Yeah, the baby is walking!"...I said my first word, "Yeah, the baby is talking!" Every milestone: the baby is going to school; the baby is graduating, the baby got her doctorate; the baby got a promotion—they celebrated. Seeing Barbara do "big things" just became an unspoken norm. My family simply loved me. Though they were genuine in their doting, the constant admiration left me addicted to the approval of others; on an endless search for external affirmation and a closeted perfectionist. I found myself constantly needing people to affirm me; to tell me how well I did, how good I looked, or how much I inspired them to be better. I suffered from what I refer to as the pedestal syndrome—high on the pedestal is where people would automatically place me. I did not solicit this position, gave no indication that I wanted to be there, and struggled to keep my balance atop such a narrow surface.

DEEPER Women™ Teach

This need for the praise and approval of others and the need to have things just perfect established in me an overwhelming, negative belief. If no one was clapping, I felt that what I did or who I was just was not worthy of the stage. Though these were my private thoughts, this often showed up in my behavior—in my life choices. I had become so dependent on the value that other people assigned to me that I stayed in an unhealthy marriage, had developed a toxic relationship with my career, and constantly found myself doing things that I did not want to do to please people who I knew did not like me. The INSANITY of it all is baffling!

By examining my life and identifying the root cause of negative behaviors, I was able to regain custody of myself. I was able to take my power back from the perception of people and positions and give it to purpose!

Go DEEPER:

For me, the addiction to external affirmation and validation kept my feet nailed to the ground for far too long. What is it for you? What is keeping you tethered to a place where you no longer belong? Examine the patterns of behavior that may be impeding your progress. What is emerging as the thing that is holding you back? Take some time to sit with yourself and search the origin of the behavior. Process your thinking in the DEEPER Thinking Space below:

_____

_____

_____

_____

_____

_____

_____

_____

DEEPER Women™ Teach

Eliminate the Barriers—

The process of examining my life helped me stop blaming people, other entities, or ideals, and prompted me to fix my focus on me. With this new awareness of the addiction to external affirmation, I needed to break the addiction and adopt new behaviors. I had to establish, what I like to call, "replacement thoughts or replacement behaviors". When I would feel the need to please or the urge to hold on to something, I would ask myself a few questions: What am I feeling? Where is this coming from? Is this a feeling or is it a fact? Why am I holding on to this? How is it serving me?

Taking just a few minutes to consider these questions completely shifted how I approach challenges in my life and my role as a leader; more specifically, how I address life-changing events as they occur in the middle of my leadership.

As a part of the divorce, I had to sell the marital property and purchase a new home. I loved our family home;

at least that is what I told myself. When I asked myself the question, "How does it serve me?" I was blown away at my response. The house no longer served me. I did not need it in the same way—the way that I did when it was purchased as a marital property and a place to raise our children. The truth was, at approximately 5600 square feet, located in a premier community, the house represented status for me. I liked what it represented at the time of purchase and how it looked to other people. The other truth, we were drowning in debt trying to keep up with the mortgage and the appearance. We had nearly perfect credit, but that was only proof that we paid our debts on time. We lived far above our means and suffered because of it; even though we would not admit it.

So, when it was time for me to purchase a new home, I was determined to begin living below my means, rid myself of debt, become financially secure, and live, lead, and model the life I wanted for myself.

DEEPER Women™ Teach

I am out of the marriage, but still a leader in my career. However, it no longer leads me. I now have a healthy relationship with it; giving it discretionary time and energy. It is not all of who I am. My identity is independent of it. It is what I do…period. It is not WHO I am.

Ironically, my marriage and my career had become barriers in my life. The more energy I gave them, the more they took…the bigger they became. The two things that I thought were propelling me had actually become an albatross around my neck. Neither of them were serving me the way they once did; so it was time I stopped worshipping them. Determined not to relapse, as a general practice, (when I am up against it) I constantly ask the questions that I mentioned previously: What am I feeling? Where is this coming from? Is this a feeling or is it a fact? Why am I holding on to this? How is it serving me?

Go DEEPER:

Consider some of the negative thought patterns or behaviors you have uncovered while you were examining your life. What are you doing to interrupt the pattern? What replacement thoughts or behaviors have or can you adopt and use regularly? Record them in the DEEPER Thinking Space and refer to them often.

_____

_____

_____

_____

_____

_____

_____

_____

_____

Plan Specific Action Steps—

I found many women, just like me on this path; who did not have the emotional tools or resources to deal with the grief in a way that was productive. I often found myself sharing my story of breaking down and my moments of breaking through. Seeing themselves reflected in my situation brought them hope; seeing myself in them, gave me peace.

I knew that it was a part of my journey to help other women walk boldly, brilliantly, and beautifully in their own purpose. It was important to create the space to breathe, think, write, speak, and focus on my health so that I could be "available" for them. With the distractions of the divorce and shifts in my career, I knew I would need support to stay focused on my goals. I put my leadership skills to work and put together my team. I began seeing a therapist to help me manage my emotions and support my girls. I hired a realtor who was responsible for the sale of the marital property and getting me into my new home; learned the value of FaceTime to keep the lines of communication open with my college freshman; hired a mentor to help me with my new business; and got myself a writing coach!

I literally cleared an area in my home and claimed it as "MINE"…and marked it as such. I committed to writing my first book. I bought a special journal specifically for this process. In it, I included a weekly schedule of days and times that I would dedicate to writing, a section for goal setting, and a place to record weekly assessments of my progress. My writing coach provided guidance and helped me to grow and develop as a writer.

Go DEEPER:

Perhaps you are thinking, I cannot afford to hire all of those people…or who could not reach their goals with all those resources? Trust me, when you decide what you want, you gain clarity of vision. Once you are clear, there is very little that can stop you! Once you get in action, you will get creative about how to acquire the resources. Start with writing down what you have decided. Start asking yourself these questions: What do I need to get started? Whom do I know that can help me? What resources do I already have to get what I want?

_____

_____

_____

_____

_____

_____

DEEPER Women™ Teach

Evaluate Your Progress—

I had done the work! I decided, examined, eliminated, established a plan of action, and now…How is that working for you? I wanted to stay on track and needed to be intentional about evaluating my progress along the way. If I was going to create the conditions for perpetual success, I had to adopt a system that would answer that question. I needed a systematic way to evaluate my progress along the way. As I worked to find the most effective way to monitor and adjust my action steps, I began to examine some of my current practices in my role as leader and life coach. There were certain processes that I used unconsciously and I thought starting there would give me a clue as to how to evaluate and monitor my personal progress. I needed something simple; easy to use and readily applicable. I started paying close attention to how I did everything; from cleaning my house, processes that I would follow at work, and practices that I would use to get results with my coaching clients.

DEEPER Women™ Teach

I landed on this simple, four-step process that I would use every week when I sat down to evaluate the progress toward my goals.

Step 1: REVIEW—I knew that I wanted to use my story, and my gift to help others see things differently, to support women who lead navigate life-changing events as the happened right in the middle of their leadership. Reviewing my vision kept me thinking and acting in that direction.

Step 2: REFLECT—One of my goals was to tell my story to free other women. I decided to share my story in a book. As a part of my healing process, I started journaling my thoughts for the purpose of turning the journal entries into a book. I was sure to make time to write at least 30 minutes a day to accomplish this goal. Each week, I would reflect on the goals to ensure that my actions aligned with what I said I wanted to do.

Step 3: REVISE or REPLACE—when I would assess my writing progress, if I found that I was not meeting my weekly writing goals, I would examine my actions to see what behaviors were impeding my progress and made the necessary adjustments. If there was no need for adjustments, I kissed myself!

Step 4: REPEAT—I would engage in this process every single week. This is a process that I continue to use (for myself and in my coaching and leadership training practice) as a way to help other leaders achieve perpetual success.

The weekly evaluation of my goals and actions really worked to keep me on target. No matter what I found when I looked back, I was always pleased because I knew exactly what I needed to do to regroup and reengage in the process. My goal was to write to inspire, but no matter what your goal is, an intentional evaluation process is essential. Not only in

DEEPER Women™ Teach

your goal setting, but in your supportive actions and strategies as well. You have to develop a systematic way of evaluating your progress. Be intentional!

Go DEEPER:

Think about what you want for your life? What is your vision? What goals and action steps have you established in order to get what you want? Are your behaviors aligned with your vision and goals? What adjustments do you need to make?

_____

_____

_____

_____

_____

_____

_____

_____

_____

_____

DEEPER Women™ Teach

Realize That You Can Do It!—

The divorce and the demotion have proven to be the most painfully rewarding experiences I have had. They provided the outside pressure I needed to begin examining what was really happening on the inside. The brokenness helped me to put the pieces back together in the way that they were designed to fit.

After consistently and intentionally applying these strategies, I have been able to reach my goals and begin creating the life that I want. As you may have read in my bio, in a period of six months, I was divorced and demoted, bought a house, sold my marital home, sent a child off to college, and started a life and leadership coaching and training business—helping women in leadership transition through life changing events that occur right in the middle of their leadership! Frankly, I would not have been able to create the life that I want without stated, intentional processes that I employ on a consistent basis.

I am not sure of where you are right now. I do not know the struggles you are facing or what is keeping you from living the life you want. I do know that anything that you can imagine for yourself is microscopic, compared to your true capacity for "becoming". You have always had the power!

Go DEEPER:

Sometimes we get so lost in doing the work that we do not recognize that we have already done the work. Be careful to celebrate your successes. Take time to reflect during your daily quiet time. Keep a record of the things you are accomplishing. Honor yourself by celebrating who you are becoming in the process. Acknowledge and applaud the work you have done. Realize that you can do it!

_____

_____

_____

_____

_____

_____

_____

_____

DEEPER Women™ Teach

From Struggle Comes Strength

By Dr. Leona Allen

DEEPER Women™ Teach

July 22, 2012—my 41st birthday. I had had enough. I was the mother of two boys, struggling with running a practice and unhappily married. I was overweight at a whopping 205 pounds. Although my weight was down from 225 pounds, I barely recognized myself. I had managed to lose 20 pounds after the birth of my first child; yet, I was struggling to shed the other 50. No matter what I did, it was just not working.

I had not known what weight trouble was until I experienced it myself. I exercised. I ate well; took my handful of supplements every day—only to realize disappointing results. The discouragement brought up those old thoughts of unworthiness and insecurity.

A Natural Healthcare Practitioner, whose purpose was to help others get healthier naturally, I could not get my own health in order. I was frustrated. I was dealing with headaches, fatigue, depression, lower back pain, and mood swings; adding to my sense of inadequacy were fear, low self-confidence, and shame. What was going on? As a doctor, I was supposed to figure out how to address such concerns. People relied on me to help them overcome their list of health issues. I had to confess—deep down inside, I felt apprehensive, because I was unable to help myself. Yes, I admit. I was embarrassed and ashamed and started to doubt myself as a doctor.

Nevertheless, I got through the days wearing my "mask". Very few people had any idea what I was going through. I plastered that smile on my face, and kept going; even when it felt like I was carrying the weight of the world on my shoulders. I was depressed and cried myself to sleep almost every night.

How the Journey Began

That day, my birthday, something came over me. As I gazed at myself in the mirror, I was able to look beyond my current circumstances and myself. I began to see that there was something more to that person staring back at me. I was ready to find her. Once I made up my mind to go DEEPER, my journey to freedom began. I had to get my health back.

I knew I had to figure this out. I knew that if I did not get my weight under control, I was likely to develop heart disease, cancer, or diabetes, just like many others in my family. I had seen what these illnesses could do to the body, and I did not want it to happen to me. I embarked on a mission to find answers. I knew I had a lot at stake. I came to the point that I had to heal my body not just for my sake, but also for the sake of my children.

Once I made the decision to change my circumstances, I noticed opportunities that helped to guide me on my journey. Initially, my journey started with wanting to lose weight, but over time, my health and my life evolved in ways I could have never imagined.

DEEPER Women™ Teach

I began to learn more about functional nutrition and how it related to human physiology. I started to learn about healing at the cellular level and understand more about getting to the source of the problem and not just addressing the symptoms. Contrary to popular belief and all the weight loss myths, I increased my fat intake and significantly reduced my intake of inflammatory foods, such as grains and sugars. I was intrigued, to say the least, the more I studied and researched the topic. I started recommending these practices in my office and the course of my nutrition and wellness programs began to change for the better. I lost almost twenty pounds within six months. I was ecstatic! Not only was I losing weight again, my energy levels increased, and my headaches were gone. Then for the next three months, the weight loss stopped. Nothing was changing. Nothing at all. I thought I was on to something, only to remain stuck for months on end.

DEEPER Women™ Teach

The struggle was real! I had hit a plateau. I was so discouraged that I lost my enthusiasm and almost gave up. Up to this point, I had done my best to make all the right decisions. Now, it seemed as if everything started to spiral downward. Instead of focusing on my success, my focus shifted to my failures.

This stage is important to understand. This is where people usually get discouraged and where many of us give up. I believe it would be safe to assume that most of us have felt discouraged at one time or another. Discouragement happens with unmet expectations. Feeling discouraged can lead to feelings of hopelessness, confusion, anger, fear, and boredom. This is the stage where, instead of letting overwhelming emotions defeat you, digging DEEPER and analyzing why you may be feeling this way become crucial.

Typically, I tend to be hard on myself, especially when things do not work out as anticipated. I had been at this stage so many times before, and every time, it feels like the world is going to end. It feels like, no matter what I do, nothing works. These times of failure numb us. We become our own worst enemy; demonstrating self-sabotaging behavior. Despite our good intentions, we eventually end up where we started. We might feel unable to get further in life. Willpower and discipline fail us. We ask ourselves, What now?

The answer to moving forward lies in understanding our self-limiting beliefs. Our beliefs directly impact our choices, behaviors, and actions. We need to evaluate those beliefs, which subconsciously, prevent us from getting what we want. My negative reactions to my struggles were a direct result of my negative thoughts. My thoughts produced the feelings of unworthiness; not being good enough, undeserving of love and success; and feeling inadequate—all led me to actions that supported those beliefs. Despite my best efforts over the years, I ultimately ended up in a life that supported those core beliefs. It did not matter how many degrees I had, or the exotic vacations I took, the house I lived in, or the clothes I wore. My healing required changing my thoughts.

A Matter of Beliefs

The source of my negative beliefs could be traced to my childhood. Unfortunately, these negative beliefs played repeatedly in my mind for years. By the time I reached adulthood, I had been programmed to make decisions and take action deeply roots in my beliefs. For years, I engaged in self-sabotaging behavior; and I just could not figure out why. I repeatedly ended up in the same type of mess! Every time it happened, it felt worse and worse. It began to take a toll on my health.

During my weight loss journey, there were those familiar moments when I was stuck and got discouraged. It was during those moments that I learned the most about myself. I had to become bigger than the challenges. That is when it all started to click. Many people give up because their expectations to lose weight are not being met. They do not believe in their bodies' true innate ability to heal, or they do not have the right support system, the right knowledge, or the right mindset. This experience taught me that in order to see the results I wanted, I had to trust and be patient with the healing process. I stopped believing in the illness and began believing in the healing. It was only then that I began healing at a DEEPER level. It was only then that I realized that not only did I have to focus on healing my body; I had to heal my mind. As I healed my mind, I began to heal my body.

Here is the truth: What we think is what we believe. What we believe is who we become. I had spent a great majority of my life believing I was not good enough; I was not important enough, or not worthy enough. So, I had become someone who did not push herself, settled for less, or gave up easily. These beliefs were based on negative events or what someone else thought of me. I realized that what someone else thinks of me does not define me.

Change Your Thoughts, Change Your Life

Since you become what you believe, you must learn to align your thoughts with strong empowering thoughts. When you change your thoughts, you change your life. As I continued in my journey, this became more than just looking good in my clothes. This evolved more into changing my inner world. Once I changed my mindset, I began to deal with my fears, doubts, and disbeliefs that were holding me back. I noticed how my state of health was directly proportional to my state of mind. I started to ensure that I took steps in the direction that would bring me closer to health and wellness and away from sickness and disease. I focused on establishing the right patterns and creating new, healthier thoughts and habits. My journey became about becoming happier, becoming confident, and being able to love myself and embrace the life that I had, and those in it.

What are some of the limiting beliefs that have been holding you back? Here are some examples of beliefs I have experienced, and some that I have heard from clients:

-Things never work out for me.

-I do not have the money.

-I have too much going on.

-I am not a morning person.

-I do not have enough time.

-This is too difficult for me.

-I am not good enough.

Here is a bit of advice: Do not believe the lies! It is possible to change these old beliefs. During your journey, it is important to monitor your thoughts daily, and start to replace those negative, self-limiting beliefs with more affirming thoughts. That is where I started. I began to visualize myself at my ideal weight. Soon, I felt an abundance of energy that I did not have before. I continued to immerse myself in learning about health, listening to audio recordings, reading books, and spending time with like-minded people. I went back to the gym. I had to fill my mind with what I wanted—counteracting what I did not.

You cannot think positive and negative thoughts simultaneously. If a self-limiting belief comes to your mind, remove it right away and replace it with a supportive belief. For example, if the self-limiting belief, "I am always tired!" comes up, think about what it would feel like to have an abundance of energy. What would you do with that energy? Visualize what you want as though it were happening. Create a new belief statement, such as, "My body is getting stronger every day!"

DEEPER Women™ Teach

It is amazing how quickly your body responds to the new thought. It takes practice, but once you master it, you will see your life and your health transform.

Don't Give Up

Most of my disappointments have come from giving up too soon, and most of my successful moments have come after I persisted through the struggle. Sometimes what you see on the other side of the struggle is better than what you ever imagined. I have found this stage to be where I learned the most about myself and who I can become. I now welcome challenges, and instead of believing that they will defeat me, I embrace them, knowing that something rewarding is on the other side. Once I achieve one goal, I move on to the next; adjusting when necessary. For example, when I was 205 pounds, my first goal was to get under 200 pounds. When I hit 199 pounds, my next goal was to get to the 180s. It is so much more manageable to set up smaller goals and celebrate your successes along the way. Stay focused on the journey instead of the outcome. Refuse to beat yourself up if you find yourself off track. Instead, just stop and evaluate your thoughts.

Remember, struggle does not equal failure. You must not confuse your struggles with failure. Look at your struggles as a test, and a chance to assess and reevaluate. Instead of giving up when things get tough, this is the best time to reflect on why it is occurring. Occasionally, you will want to return to your old habits because they were more "comfortable." You remember how much easier it was to go to the drive-through versus cooking a whole meal. That is human nature. The good news is you can create new habits. This is the time to be creative. Reach out to others who are doing similar things and share ideas. I encourage you to find a friend or a health coach to go through this journey with you. We all go through this cycle of challenges. Do not look at it as failure. It is a part of the growth process in developing a healthier lifestyle. Trust the process and never give up…on yourself.

Your Journey to FREEDOM

The key is to keep going. Get comfortable with being uncomfortable. From your struggle comes your strength. Do not give up. Remember why you started in the first place. Monitor your thoughts daily and stay focused on the process. Be patient. Learn from your mistakes and celebrate your wins along the way. You've got this!

DEEPER Women™ Teach

Take a moment to go **DEEPER** and reflect on your journey:

What do you want to change the most about your health and why?

DEEPER Women™ Teach

Do you believe you can change the course of your health?

What do you think has been stopping you from achieving your health and/or weight loss goals?

_____

_____

_____

_____

_____

_____

_____

_____

_____

_____

_____

_____

_____

_____

DEEPER Women™ Teach

List at least three self-limiting beliefs that tend to come up most frequently when you are ready to give up or even refuse to start (for example, not enough energy or not enough time).

_____

_____

_____

_____

_____

_____

_____

_____

_____

_____

_____

_____

_____

_____

DEEPER Women™ Teach

Now, tap into the inner winner in you. List at least three wins that have occurred in your life in the last six months. What did you overcome to experience the wins?

_____

_____

_____

_____

_____

_____

_____

_____

_____

_____

_____

Welcome to the DEEPER Life! Apply these principles and you will achieve more FREEDOM in your health, your life, and in your leadership! Be well.

Your results are a reflection of your actions.

If you take no action, expect no results.

If you take inconsistent action, expect inconsistent results.

If you take focused, inspired, unstoppable action, expect your dreams to come true.

-Dr. Leona Allen

DEEPER Women™ Teach

Broken to be Blessed

By Pamela Dingle

DEEPER Women™ Teach

I was placed on a corrective action plan for the first time in my 30-year career and assigned a mentor who asked me what I needed to work on. Why would a "skilled leader" have to ask what I need to work on? If an employee needs a corrective action, a "skilled leader"—assigned as my mentor—should be able to clearly identify the gap and articulate the strategies needed to remediate the areas of concern. This was the final straw! I would no longer play this game!

There comes a time in life that we find ourselves holding on the vestiges of precious experiences that were never meant to be ours forever; this was definitely one of these moments for me. The beaten pathway I was on began to reimagine itself, and I was completely oblivious to the change.

I started this journey about five years ago, not knowing that my expectations were redefining themselves, and I would no longer feel the warmth of my day-to-day existence or recognize that I was on a path to a new and unimagined world. It started rather abruptly with a series of life changes that catapulted me into a new reality. The love of my life walked out while he was in the middle of a health crisis simply stating, "I don't think I really want to try to work on this relationship."—when pressed about whether he had found a counselor that he liked well enough to guide us through this hard journey we were up against.

The sting of these words left me paralyzed for days. My feet felt like they were mired in mud and I was trying desperately to move them and put up a false air of fortitude and strength—I was failing miserably. My thoughts began to swirl as I tried to formulate some type of question to force a conversation that should have been held in a more respectful manner; instead of speaking through a wall with an opening to the kitchen—me on one side and him on the other. Responding to his remark, I think I stammered out something unintelligible. This characterized our pattern of communication—he would tell me what he wanted, I would swallow it, and my own hopes and dreams to support him through a perpetual state of crisis. This communication was completely inadequate to sustain a relationship.

It has been said that behind every good leader, there is someone that encourages, inspires, motivates and yes, even restores their resolve when the avalanche of challenges cascades down on them. In the beginning, this was my former husband. He did this for me. He would sweep me away from the worries and cares of hungry or vulnerable children and adults who seemingly got in their own way through resistance and pride. I could count on being able to get away from it all; come home, prepare a meal and have conversation and snuggle into the safety that my marriage afforded me. In that moment, my foundation had crumbled and the irreparable crack made supporting it unsustainable. Even more devastating, I was left with a monumental load of debt, few resources and no support. I struggled to keep everything afloat as I supported our daughter and maintained our existence, paid for my education as I was finishing my last graduate degree and tried to keep the composed front needed to survive in my current job.

This devastating departure came at a time when I had transitioned into one of the most challenging leadership roles of my life, Director of Curriculum in one of the largest school districts in the United States. After encouragement from a couple of my colleagues, I decided to move forward. I accepted the position. I sincerely and genuinely enjoyed working to inspire people to come together; synergizing their incredible talents, passion, and energy—creating a cohesive, progressive approach to supporting the needs of the district.

This new journey was not without some enormous challenges. Within 120 days, my supervisor changed three times and each had extremely different personalities and approaches. The style of our leader, at that time, was vastly different from those who led before with the high touch, engaged interactive approaches; inspiring leaders through their sense of presence and placing knowledgeable iconic leaders in key roles. This leader skulked about like a vapor making covert appearances and calling in plays from a hidden vantage point. Were it not for the initial connections, one would have thought that he was merely a figment of the imagination, some mysterious voice calling in plays from a well-developed playbook. For whatever reason, he left almost as abruptly as he had arrived; creating, yet another transition in leadership and a new vision.

When the new leader of the organization was announced, there was an air of stunned silence. There were so many other qualified candidates and he initially lacked the minimal qualifications for the position. Eventually, we were summoned to hear from our new leader, and I reported with anxious thoughts and a desire to lay the swirling rumors to rest. I was literally numb from the frequent shifts; hoping that this new chapter would bring some sort of stabilization. I entered the auditorium to which we had been summoned, I blocked out the speculations about what was ahead, tried to select the right seat to be distant from the other onlookers, and prepared myself for what was to come.

Anxiety slowly invaded. I felt something just did not seem right about this moment. Soon the new leader walked out with a confident gait, planted himself in the middle of the stage; standing confidently with an air of arrogance. He began with a brief tale intended to loosen up the audience; I just could not find my sense of humor, which rarely evades me, at that moment. As he stood pouring out his vision for the future—"We will NOT be moving education into the 21st century learning; we will be returning to who we once were." I could not imagine why we would do that and what it would look like. As the leader helping to shape our forward movement, I felt like this message was directed towards me as my team and I had been leading the charge to prepare students for what lies ahead and encouraging others to think differently about what education would look like. I could not seem to catch my breath for a second. I had to reassure myself that I had not gotten a direct "eye" during this unnerving introduction. I just sat with a stunned look hiding under an artificial supportive tone.

I left pretty immediately that day with a foreboding sense about the message that was clearly delivered, but the worst of this transition had not even begun to be unfurled!

As if our organization had not been destabilized enough, the newly selected Cabinet Leaders would be comprised of some leaders with limited leadership experience for the roles they were assuming. This was challenging for an organization that had already gone through numerous leadership shifts. The forward direction would feel turbulent like drifting in a small boat on a wind-tossed sea. My thoughts were reeling as I tried to absorb the implications of the changes. I attempted to reassure myself that everything would be alright though I knew this was not a promising scenario.

My suspicions were validated almost immediately during our leadership launch that year. The team that I supervised was noticeably shifted and my job title revamped; sending a clear message of impending trouble. I was strongly recommended to leave the role I was in and move to safety in a different department to avoid the fray. I was again reassigned to a new team and warned by several that this move would position me for future challenges. My new team seemed a little on edge and there was a hush among colleagues who knew something was amiss.

I made an internal commitment to focus on the work to be done, hid away with my team as much as possible, and found solace in the opportunity to work in my element once again—supporting the most vulnerable population of the district—children from diverse socio-economic backgrounds. This worked for a brief period until the plan for me was rolled out. I had colleagues come to tell me to "watch my back" or "I'm trying to get them to leave you alone". Leave me alone? What was my crime, introducing schools to a means of educating students that would effectively prepare them for the future? The attacks intensified as time progressed with false accusations, private conversations with members of my team recording meetings, altered documents—finally began to wear me down as I argued over how the work would be executed, how schools would be supported, and how we would complete our work. I would go to leadership meetings and isolate myself as best I could for the protection of others; as anyone who aligned himself or herself with me would surely face harsh consequences. I went home exhausted each night and had to spend 30-40 minutes in spiritual renewal. I would repeat this practice each morning—just to go to work. The chaos of looming threats and uncertainty of it all, left me worried and anxious all of the time. Where was my safe place? No solace at home…no peace at work.

DEEPER Women™ Teach

I was ultimately asked to meet with the district Executive HR leadership near the end of the second year and told I had not met the tenets of the undefined corrective action plan put hastily in place about a month prior to the meeting. I was assured the false charge that had been "trumped up" would be destroyed and was then given an untenable offer to go back to lead a school because I was "valued" by the organizational leader. Since my experiences did not match those words, I wrote a historical summary of my experiences with the district and the incredible fortuity, promotions, and growth opportunities I had been afforded in my 23 years, left it with a somewhat nervous HR Executive whose parting words were, "I was told you were a woman of grace; now I see what everyone means". I said good-bye, with sincere and genuine gratitude for all I had been allowed to do—realizing this experience helped shape me for what was next.

Today I work with some of the most talented, passionate, and equipped leaders who are shaping new frontiers for students through creativity and innovation. I am daily inspired by their tenacity and perseverance to work around financial obstacles, shortage of resources, sometimes low-motivation or engagement of effort. I watch them catalyze changes in the lives of students and communities and am learning each day more and more about what good leadership looks like and accomplishes.

Lessons for Leaders

Shift Your Perspective- I realized that I needed to change my thought patterns. There is a poem by an early 20th century poet that says, "If you think you're beaten, you are." When you allow your thoughts to settle into hopelessness, they literally become the force that brings defeat and your perspective of powerlessness.

One morning as I lay in bed meditating and praying, I heard very clearly, "Do you think they are more powerful than I am?" A sense of shame washed over me and coursed through my weariness. I had been talking to God about my problem. Now, it was time to tell my problem about my God.

I am so grateful to have been able to nestle into a higher power that saw me through a period when loneliness and abandonment almost pulled me under like an oceanic undertow. Then clarity washed in like a gentle tide. I no longer needed to live in this space of intense stress and uncertainty. I simply would no longer play this game! I was steeled by the reassurance that I was more valuable than I was being treated and had developed a cadre of skills that could be utilized in any number of situations which in essence is what I was reminded of by my mentor.

Sometimes we find ourselves in difficult situations and in mining the reasons search from within for a reason or blame. While this is a good place to begin because we always need to be reflective and cultivate or refine ourselves, the circumstances in which you find yourself are not always of your doing. More importantly, we need to understand that not every situation is the right one for the talents, skills or gifts of a leader, some are simply not worthy or lack the cultural alignment to your gifts.

Examine your perspective, shift your narrative, and rewrite your story which likely sounds like a scratched record skipping over and over the same thoughts needing a gentle nudge forward. (If you are under 50 years of age, talk to someone older). I shifted mine to understand that I was guided by a much higher power who knew the end from the beginning, the plan that He had for me, and no Goliath, or powerful individual, truly has the ability to destroy what is designed for my future. (If you love a great story, read about David, a shepherd boy with a bag of stones who defeats Goliath, a giant who was shrouded with weapons and an armor. This story is found in the Bible in I Samuel 17. Remember that whatever you think about yourself is what you will ultimately become. (Jeremiah 29:11; Isaiah 46:9-10; Psalms 23:7)

DEEPER Women™ Teach

Quiet the Noise-Each morning I would awaken and lie in bed listening to spiritual music and a brief sermon for the day. This would prepare me for anything I would face, but it also brought a sense of peace and joy within. Intentionally set aside quiet time preferably before the day begins to focus your thoughts, feed your mind, and spirit a healthy diet to "armor up" for the day. This will chase away the noise and arm you with the fortitude needed to walk on stormy seas with a peace that surpasses all understanding of your situation. You may even need to carry with you small affirmations or scriptures that serve as a shield and keep you encouraged throughout the day to combat the onslaught of projectiles hurled at you from multiple or unexpected directions.

Employ mindfulness strategies. Utilize breathing techniques. Listen to soothing music. These are all ways to bring a sense of peace and calm despite what is going on around you. Finally, laugh on purpose! Laugh with friends and family, laugh at comedy specials, laugh at yourself, but use the power of laughter to release the great neurotransmitters that make you feel good. By the way, there are other ways to release these powerful chemicals just make sure you're doing so in a thoughtful way!

(*Psalms 46:10*; *Philippians 4:6-7*)

When we are going through storms, the sound of the winds and the waves beating viciously upon the boat that we are in distracts us from the voice that should be resonating through our minds. We need to create intentional opportunities to silence the distractions to hear the still, small voice that is piloting us to safety. Jeremiah 29:11 says, "For I know the plans that I have for you," declares the Lord, "plans to prosper you and not to harm you, plans to give you hope and a future." Recognize that no one can co-opt the plan for your future. No one can hinder your purpose but you. "Cease striving!" and cancel the evil narrative writing itself in your mind. This narrative externally infused into your psyche—it is up to you to cancel its effectiveness.

Rewrite Your Narrative-It is essential that you begin to rewrite your narrative once your mind is settled and clear. Who do *you* want to be? Where do *you* want to use your talents and gifts? What is *your purpose,* in other words, what did God place you here on this earth to accomplish for *His* glory? It is essential in this step to surround yourself with the right voices, those that build your armor and speak the same language like a friend who advised me to, "*Stand up!*". These people will encourage you, pray for you, and feed you in a way that replenishes what is being stolen from you each day.

Seek direction from God and know when it is His timing for you to move forward and embrace the changes needed or ask Him to help you see your capabilities which are under attack. As long as our minds are focused on the voices pointing out the negatives or the absurdities of our situations, we remain in a spiraling story that grows and may lead to victimization, but when we shift our perspective and get still, we can reflect on what we have that has been leading us to our destiny.

Start writing the lessons you have learned, the skills you possess, the accomplishments of your efforts, and what you feel you can do with the gifts with which you have been equipped. You will be amazed at the options that are ahead for you. Stephen Covey admonishes us in, Seven Habits of Highly Effective People, to "Begin with the end in Mind". Write out your vision and map out where you see yourself in the upcoming year, in five years, in ten years and include specific action steps and *S.M.A.R.T.* goals (Specific, Measurable, Attainable, Reasonable and Time-bound), training that you need or mentors that you should invite to be a part of your story. Do not be afraid to dream BIG! Nothing is accomplished by dreaming small.

Identify leaders who can inspire or influence your direction. There are so many with powerful stories that can assist you in this stage.

DEEPER Women™ Teach

*Take the Next Steps-*When you have a clear plan of action, begin to build your leadership arsenal by reading the works of leaders in the field like *Simon Sinek's Start with Why* where we learn how some leaders are able to inspire others and achieve great things together. Another good read is Tom Rath and Barry Conchie's *Strengths Based Leadership*. Make sure that you are aware of your strengths, so you can take them to the organization that will most benefit from what you have to offer. Read anything that John Maxwell has written! *Attitude 101, Failing Forward, 21 Laws of Indisputable Leadership,* and *Winning with People* are just a few of my favorites. I believe John Maxwell has some 80+ titles. You can win with any of them. Begin to grow your thinking as you take the next step.

This step may be the scariest of all if you have committed your time and talents to something for several years, however, your circumstances will clearly let you know when it is time to move forward especially if you have followed the steps of mapping out your vision and creating S.M.A.R.T. goals. You will likely see the disconnect in where you are and the direction in which you should be headed. Remember to leave any situation better than you found it if it is at all possible; your legacy is built as much through your departure as it is when you are in a situation. Show grace to your accusers, attackers, or foes. Silence is often grace. Do not diminish who you are by cow-towing to their low-level tactics. Let your strength and fortitude be your final statement. Always keep Proverbs 3:5-6 in mind, "Trust in the Lord with all your heart…and He shall direct your path."

DEEPER Women™ Teach

DEEPER Thinking Space:

What part of this story resonated with you the most?

_____
_____
_____
_____
_____
_____
_____

Have you ever come under unjust fire as a woman who leads?

_____
_____
_____
_____
_____
_____
_____

DEEPER Women™ Teach

How did you handle it? What did you do to resolve the issue?

Who Is Sleeping With Your Husband?

My Journey to Healing

By Jeri Godhigh

DEEPER Women™ Teach

I don't know what I need, but I know I need something…I cannot keep living like this. These were the words that I uttered to my new Life and Leadership Coach during our Discovery Call. I was so confused by my state. As the owner of a successful real estate company, who had recently taken the leap to expand my entrepreneurial venture to include an insurance company; although both companies were doing really well, I was miserable. Though business was booming, life at home was deflating. I felt like my husband and I were in a stuck place in our marriage and I did not know how to fix it. I was leading in business, but losing at home.

I started the session by explaining how I could not keep my house clean. I complained that my husband was not helping me with chores…how he needed to spend more time with our son…how he needed to help me cook; we needed to be on the same page—the list of complaints went on and on. My coach asked me a question that would set me squarely on the path to me. She asked, "So, Jeri...where do you fit into all of this?" This made me turn my sight right where it needed to be—on me.

As far back as I can remember; as far back as a little girl, I lacked self-esteem. My weight was never just right, my hair was not straight enough, I did not believe I had any talent, and I struggled with my self-worth. This made me overdo, over give, overthink, over attach; and over depend on other people to give me just as I had given to them. I was exhausted and now, I had nothing left to give. This left me feeling lost, empty, and unfulfilled. I was in a bad place. It was not my marriage that was stuck, it was I.

My father passed away when I was just five years old. Until this period of my life, I had not thought about it deeply enough to unpack the low self-esteem and self-doubt. Dr. JoAnn Deak, Psychologist and Author, conveys that a girl's self-esteem and self-confidence largely comes from the father. Without having a consistent father (or father figure) in my life, I felt like I had not fully developed. I just did not have the confidence in who I was or understood what I had to offer. I kept looking to my husband to fill my "daddy void".

I never knew that my husband could not fulfill every part of me. I depended, solely, on him to make me happy—to fill the gaps in my life. I kept expecting him to do something that he just did not have the capacity to do. He could not fill the void created by the loss of my father. He could not meet my every need; he could not be my all in all. He could not heal my "daddy wound". That responsibility belonged to me. Only me. I had to fix it. I had to find me.

This is where my journey to authenticity began. It was time that I found out who I really was—what, on earth, was my purpose in life? I was determined not leave this earth without having accomplished the very things God created me to do.

DEEPER Women™ Teach

I began to see how I could crawl my way of the box I had been in all of my life. My insecurities limited me. Life inside the box meant that I was fine and content to live a routine life. I had to push myself to get out of the box. To re-envision how I wanted to live. I started working on renewing my mind; changing the way that I thought about myself. I had to get out of the Box!

When I started looking for me, there were a few steps that I needed to take.

Investigate. I had to dig deep to get to the root and find the source of the hurt. I had lived with this for years and knew that I could not do this alone. So, I got help. I sought a life coach and a licensed therapist. Through this process, I was able to focus primarily on me and my role and responsibility for my own happiness. No, I could not change the past, but I could certainly move forward in a different way. I had to come to the understanding that the holes I was trying to fill could only be filled by the one who created me—

God. Understanding my origin helped me to grasp the fact that I was worth it; just because. I did not have to overdo anything anymore. In the absence of an earthly father, I found God the Father to be my everything; my all in all.

We must put our hope and trust in the Lord knowing we have a purpose here on earth. Purpose gives meaning. It provides you solid foundations. So when life does not always go as planned, understanding your purpose helps to ground you; reminds you of just who you are. When we have defined our purpose in life, we can hold steady during the trying times of storms and doubt.

Announcement-I decided that I had had enough. The low self-esteem, the not feeling worthy, and the over focusing on my body was done. It was time that I started telling myself who I was. I started telling myself something different. *I know that I am powerful—I am victorious. I can do this; and so can you.* These were just a few of the announcements.

- God has made me and blessed me! He has clothed me with His glory and has presented me as good. I am the gift!
- I am a woman of wisdom. I know what to do at the time I need to do it. I have God-given insight.
- I am fulfilling my purpose in God and fruit abounds in every area of my life.
- I am free from fear, doubt, and worry.
- I am a woman of power, great presence, high position, and prosperity

Defend- From time to time, those feelings of fear, doubt, and unworthiness rear their deceitful heads. At times, my memory lapses and I briefly forget about who I am and what I can do. When this happens, I do not just sit in it. I defend myself with my favorite scriptures or with thoughts that are more positive. I continue to walk in faith—knowing that I must stay the course because now I understand that I will surely win if I do not quit.

Set Boundaries- As I began to come into myself, I started to realize just how much of me I had given away. I had made it a practice to be the answer to everybody's problem, but nobody was there when I was the one asking the questions. People had become accustomed to getting their needs met through me. You need a committee chair…Jeri's got it; need someone to watch your children…Jeri's got it; need someone to clean up behind…Jeri's got it. Well, Jeri will not have it anymore. It was time for me to set boundaries. I had to stop giving everything to everybody and start giving for me. Don't get me wrong, I am still supportive and generous with my time and resources; however, now I give from a different place. I give from a healed place. I no longer give in exchange for validation or affirmation; I no longer give out of fear; I no longer give our of insecurity.

DEEPER Women™ Teach

Now I give if I have it; I give if I think it will add value; I give expecting nothing in return.

Plan- One of the things that I learned through my coaching program was that whatever I did to become successful in business; I had to do to become successful in other parts of my life. As a successful businesswoman, I knew how to put together a plan. I dreamed about how I wanted my business to look; I set goals and benchmarks and shared them with my staff. I brought everybody along with me. Around the third or fourth week of working with my Life and Leadership Coach, she asked, "How do your employees know the direction for your company and the work that they need to go to get there?" I responded, "I tell them…I think about what I want and then come up with a plan." She celebrated with me because I had figured it out—I needed to do the same thing for my relationships that I had to done in my business.

DEEPER Women™ Teach

I started dreaming (again) about how I wanted my marriage and family to look; about how I wanted us to live and operate as a family—considering my role in having it become exactly what I wanted it to become. I established a vision for myself, set goals, and shared them with my husband and family. I also allowed them to share what they thought and felt about what I wanted for the family. I allowed them to dream with me. Today, we are all growing together and supporting each other as we each attempt to live up our part of the vision.

Taking this journey has been one of the most challenging and rewarding endeavors I have ever undertaken in my life. This work has not been easy. I kept blaming my husband for all of the things that were wrong with our relationship...with us, and with me. I was projecting all of what I was not and assigning it to him. I made him responsible for me. That expectation came from all of the broken pieces in me and that was wrong. The misplaced expectations hurt my entire family. I am grateful that I woke up to me. Being able to see myself has helped me to see my husband more clearly. Now, I know who is sleeping with my husband, but do you know who is sleeping with yours?

DEEPER Thinking Space:

Whom have you made responsible for your life? List their names here.

_____

_____

_____

_____

_____

_____

_____

_____

_____

DEEPER Women™ Teach

For what have you made them responsible?

_____
_____
_____
_____
_____
_____
_____

Release them. Ask them for forgiveness and then forgive yourself. Now, take responsibility for your own life. Write down what you are willing to do to regain control of your life.

_____
_____
_____
_____
_____
_____
_____

DEEPER Women™ Teach

Hold On and Fight

By Lorarine Loving

DEEPER Women™ Teach

Life is a journey we all must take. Some of us start out with high, lofty dreams of living the so-called good life. As young, naïve children, we think life is easy. We think all we have to do is get a job and make lots of money. We do not think much about the downsides of life. We do not think of being disappointed—friends and family hurting us. We do not think about wrong choices and their consequences. We just think everything will fall into place.

As I began to navigate my way through life, my life actually blurred my vision. When life got tough, I changed course. When things did not go my way, I shut down. When I felt unappreciated, I lashed out. I was chasing material things when I should have been chasing God. I was looking for love and acceptance in all the wrong places. I was making decisions without Godly counsel and kept finding myself in some messed up situations. My life was stressful and unfulfilling. I was on a winding road that never went anywhere.

DEEPER Women™ Teach

In the fall of 2011, I signed up to run my first half marathon. At that time, I could barely complete a two-mile walk. Now, my plan was to train for four months in preparation for the thirteen-mile event. I would have to train five days a week. My trainer lived more than two hundred miles away. This meant that I had to encourage myself to reach my goal.

This was not an easy task. My record of accomplishments was not very good. I had quit just about everything I started. I quit piano just before becoming a virtuoso. I quit voice lessons. I quit selling Mary Kay. I quit selling Avon. I quit many jobs. I quit working in my second Master of Education Degree. I quit efforts to get healthier. I had even given up on God and the life He had blessed me to have.

Burying old habits was very difficult. I had to experience a paradigm shift. I needed to change my behavior. Even as I wrote this book, I was struggling to meet my goals.

DEEPER Women™ Teach

It has taken me ten years to take the first step toward becoming a published author. Yes, you read correctly. It has taken me ten years to put the first word to paper. That is because I allowed my old habits of poor time management to get the best of me. I made excuses not to write. In fact, I made excuses not to lead anything. I did not want to be out in front for anything. I was comparing my credentials to those of established authors and leaders. To tell the truth, I was hiding from people; and from God. I was ashamed and perceived that I had not accomplished much in my adulthood.

I knew that God had more for me. I could no longer ignore the dreams he had placed inside of me. Why hadn't the blessings started to fall? I was waiting. I was waiting on God…but he was waiting on me.

So, I had to get in action. I had to tap into the fight inside of me. I wanted it, but this was no easy task. Just like when I was training for the half marathon, I wanted to quit. I even wanted to quit while I was running the race. Halfway through the course, a bystander was holding a sign that read, "Breathe, pray, and take one step at a time." After I read that sign, I did exactly what it said. I dug deep and pushed myself. Today I am very proud of my accomplishments—the race, and penning my story for this book.

I had to fight my way to the finish line; fight for the life I know God has for me. I had to FIGHT and not give up—

- Forgive
- Intentionally Live
- Get Moving
- Have Faith
- Tired, What is that?

Forgive. Forgiveness helped me to let some things go. Somehow, I knew that I could not move forward without this step. I had to let go of the disappointments. The first person I had to forgive was myself.

This was very difficult for me. I was ashamed of some

of the choices I had made. I had lied to myself and broken so many promises to myself; because of this, I felt so unworthy. Once I began forgiving myself for wasted time and bad decision making, the process of forgiving others became easier.

One of the reasons that I had such a hard time with forgiveness was the need for closure. I had been hurt by so many; I just wanted closure. I needed to know why things ended the way they did; I wanted people to apologize and provide an explanation for their behavior. Holding on to the hurt of wrongdoing was stopping me from getting what I wanted for my life. I decided to close the door myself. I forgave. I just let it go.

Forgiveness is a choice. We can choose not to let situations or people hold us hostage. Forgiveness does not mean that we must stay in relationship or continue to engage in the situation. I like to think of it as forgive and let live.

Intentional Living. Living intentionally push me to a

life beyond merely existing. I once heard an evangelist say, "I wasn't born to live just to work, pay bills, and die." When I heard that, it ignited something deep in my soul. As a Christian, I believe that Christ came so that I may have an abundant life. Learning to live intentionally helped me to live God's purpose for my life.

I have struggled the most with this part of the FIGHT. To some extent, I still struggle. I am a self-proclaimed free spirit. I do not like rules. I do not like daily routines. I do not like strict regimens. I do not like my day scheduled down to the minute. I just want to be free and move about life as I please. So, I had to intentionally make some changes in my mindset. Living intentionally did not limit me, it freed me. I finally got a journal and used it. For years, I collected journals because they were cute or had some encouraging statement on the cover. I was distracted by the word "journal". One day I picked up a twenty-five cent, spiral notebook I had bought for my daughter, and began to write. It was in that moment that I realized that, like my life, the cover on the journal, meant nothing. What was important were the words I penned and the intentional deeds I performed to live abundantly.

While God did give us free will, He did not intend for us to make up stuff as we move through life. When we wander without goals or intentions, we find ourselves stuck; unable to achieve goals or the life we want for ourselves. We each have a purpose; God gave it to us before we were formed in our mothers' wombs. Often, He is simply waiting for us to set goals, establish a clear plan, and get in action.

It is important that you…**GET MOVING!** Setting your goals and writing your intentions are futile if you do not include specific actions in your plan. We have heard it thousands of times: *Faith without works is dead.* Intentionally Living and Get Moving are buddies. To intentionally live is to get moving. When you move, it is imperative that you know where you are going. Once you write your vision, you must do something to demonstrate your commitment to living your soul's purpose. Your actions will demonstrate to God your willingness to be used by Him. As each moment in time begins to unfold, you will begin to live life and live it abundantly.

Have Faith. No matter what is going on around you, you must have faith and know all things are working together for your good. There will be times when you have doubts. There will be times when you want to give up. You may even want to retreat and pick up old habits. You might even be fearful. Have FAITH!

I like the way Zig Ziglar described FEAR. He said, "Fear is False Evidence Appearing Real." That is exactly what fear is. You must learn to speak positively about your situations, knowing that God is working on your behalf. Be like the father in the book of Matthew who brought his son to be healed but lacked faith. He cried out to Jesus, "Lord, help my unbelief." I have heard my elders describe this type of utterance as a breath prayer. A breath prayer is short and can be said in one breath. Although it is short, the breath prayer is very powerful.

Here are a few I have used, and I know you probably have said a few of them yourself.

- Lord, help!
- Jesus!
- Have mercy, Lord!
- Touch now, Lord!
- I trust you, God!
- Protect me, Lord!
- Send your angels now, Lord!

You get the gist of it. These prayers are our emergency calls to our Heavenly Father. They have been my lifeline on many occasions. Sometimes things are happening so fast, we do not have time to think about what to say. We just know we need help. It is our faith that allows us to call out to God like this. He is always with us. He is working things out for our good.

Tired, What is That? First, let me clearly state that I will not be encouraging you to miss sleep or not to rest. I am simply saying you cannot get tired of working in your purpose. You cannot get tired of working to achieve your goals. You cannot give up on what you are supposed to do while here on earth. You cannot stop writing or telling your story. You just cannot quit on yourself or the people who are counting on your gift.

Everyday hustle and bustle can take a toll on your desire to run your race. You must remember life, indeed, a marathon. Learn how to move accordingly. Marathon runners know how to dig deep to finish a race; even when they are physically and mentally exhausted, they understand that they have more to give. They can do this because they have trained how to adjust while they are running. They know when to slow their pace, so they will not get tired. They know when to hydrate so their muscles will function correctly and not cramp. They know how to nourish the body before the race so they will have energy to complete the race. They also know how to nourish the body after the race so they can replenish and restore the body.

So, like the marathon runner, we must learn how to make these adjustments when we are working toward our dreams. Whatever you do, hold on; do not give up; rest and adjust if you must, but do not stop fighting. There is FIGHT in you.

No matter how old or young you may be, if you are inhaling and exhaling, if blood is pumping through your veins, you still have time to continue your journey. You still have time to write your story. Hold on and forgive by releasing yourself and getting over your past disappointments. Hold on to your goals and aspirations by living intentionally. Hold on and get moving by setting deadlines and being accountable to yourself. Hold on by having faith in God, the process, and yourself.

More Than The Mrs.
By Jamia Ponder

DEEPER Women™ Teach

Abandoned. Molested. Silenced. Emotionally damaged. Wounded. Bruised. Bandaged. Developmentally arrested.

Beautifully poised, positioned, and polished on the outside; yet, silencing my cries and suffocating inside. I was masked and a mess. Relishing in the ability to do it all, be it all, and achieve it all for everyone except myself. I spent most of my childhood years estranged from my biological father. Birthdays and holidays would come and go and my mind ran wild with thoughts of wonder. "I wonder if he knows it is my birthday".... "I wonder if he really cares?" I yearned to be loved, seen, and heard—considered. In an effort to cope, I learned to exchange my worth with my works. I adopted and nourished a performance-based love, using what I could accomplish as a means of validation. It was the acknowledgment that I desperately needed; coupled with the responsibility I was never meant to carry. Years went by and everyday my worth suffered a tiny blow, and I really could not tell a soul. So, I swallowed every pang—unwilling to deal with the root of the sour fruit slowly killing my beautiful tree.

Busy days and booked calendars kept me from the issues; I did not have nor did I want the time to deal with my pain. Until…it all fell apart.

At the age of 14, I got my very first job. Ah yes! The summer of 1998 was amazing! Every morning, I would excitedly dress for work and my father would drop me off on his way in to work. Up until that point, most of my summers were spent watching my younger brothers so this was a welcomed change! Soon after starting my job, I caught the attention of my 18-year-old manager and I liked it. For once, I was noticed…seen…liked. considered.

Innocent flirts quickly grew into something far outside of my control. During my shifts, I would be called away from my register, only to be cornered in back office break rooms, felt up under my shirts, and down my pants—forcefully touched. Anxiety filled my being at the thought of having to work with him. Much to his enjoyment, he would place me on all of his shifts. Every red flag was raised, but I remained silent.

Why? I asked that question myself for years. Why didn't I speak up? I guess the truth is, I liked the attention and somehow thought, if I had never entertained his advances to begin with, it would have never happened. Moreover, I did not want to lose my job so I never uttered a word; not to my parents, friends, other managers on staff…no one. I suffered; shakily working each shift until my summer job was up. It was traumatic, swallowed and soured my ability to receive an intimate touch from my spouse well over 13 years later.

I knew desired deeper intimacy with my husband, but could not figure out why HE could not understand me. I mean, I thought I was clear! Desire me, but do not put your hands on me. Be attracted to me, but do not hold me. Tell me I am beautiful, but do not overdo it—no wonder he was frustrated. It took years before I realized that I was standing in the way of the very love I desired to receive. It would be years before I realized the impact that molestation had on me; years before I acknowledged that I lived in a constant state of "triggered".

You see, to recognize the real issues, I had to come to a place of admission. I needed help. I needed love. Little Jamia was running the ship—demanding and crying out to be heard, held, and healed. She wanted to keep everything under her control because growing up, it seemed like nothing was in her control. Little Jamia was grieving; yet, not allowed to speak on it. She was hurting; yet, feeling overlooked. She suffered in silence and no one ever knew.

I purposed in my heart NOT to repeat the genetically inherited curses and determined not to transfer the impact of those errors in the lives of my children. Oh, but I was there; on the fast track to damage-city. I showed up, showed out, and that is all it was, a show. I was involved in this, chairing that; afraid to slow down because if I got still enough with my thoughts, every insecurity would come flooding in covering the room in my flaws.

That was the way it was until I hit my breaking point. I hit the end of the road. It was the last shebang. I had reached the pinnacle, the peak, the pit. I was at the point of no return. I had had enough. I mean E-damn-nuff! I could not cover it up any longer. NEWSFLASH!! If you do not deal with your mess, it will certainly deal with you!

In my very first therapy session, my counselor asked me for permission to start with two questions. The first was, "What are YOU most proud of?" The caveat she included was it had to be something I had accomplished for ME. Speechless and without an answer to her question, I nodded for her to proceed to the next question. The second question was, "Who are you?" As luck would have it, this too had a caveat. It could not be about anyone else. We all knew I was Madison, Mackenzie, and Maddox's mom and of course, we both knew I was Desmond's wife, a friend, daughter, sister but what she wanted to know had nothing to do with a linear relationship. She wanted to know who I was, and the heart wrenching, heartbreaking and earth-shattering truth was, I had absolutely NO idea. "Who are you?" were three words that shook me to my core and hit me like a ton of bricks. I did not know who I was. Everything I had done had involved someone else.

For years, I silently carried the traumas of yesteryear. I silently bore offenses. I was burying emotions. I denied myself believing the notion that somehow the silence and denial made me a better wife and mother. The truth was that I was drowning. At this point, I had been married for almost nine years to my husband who is now a 2020 medical school graduate. To offer a little history and provide a point of reference, being a physician was all my husband ever dreamed of since the first day we met. Little did I know that it would take him NINE of the THIRTEEN years that we had been together to START medical school. Nonetheless, I believed in him. Hell, I believed in him so much that I even submitted his application FOR HIM. From our first child to three children, through evictions, car repossessions, to receiving only a conditional acceptance to medical school, quitting jobs in a matter of days, coming up with insurmountable sums of money, moving abroad, surviving a catastrophic category 5 hurricane, being separated for months at a time, through a polar vortex, he finished. Within six weeks of completing medical school, COVID-19 shut everything down. Our journey to medicine has been filled with tribulations. Like any 'good' wife, I was there every step of the way! I worked multiple jobs. I Mom'ed. I volunteered. I encouraged. I pushed. I called. I scheduled. I moved. I researched. I supported. I arranged. I re-arranged. The entire time I was walking BESIDE and oftentimes in front of him every step of the way. Sound familiar?

DEEPER Women™ Teach

In May of 2020 by God's grace, he did it! He graduated medical school with High Honors. With tear-filled eyes, praising God, and rejoicing with my husband, I was thrilled. Yet simultaneously, I felt an indescribable pang because his degree was built on my back. Four years (and more) of carrying it all with seemingly nothing to show for it, I realized that it was and always would be Desmond Ponder, MD - we couldn't split that. It was not as if I would get the M and he would get the D. I am still just Mrs. Jamia Ponder.

In search of healing and surrendering all, I set out on a new journey that started with a painful admission that I was lost. I used so many other things seeking to find validation only to fall short; I never felt smart enough, talented enough, pretty enough, or wealthy enough to compete when the truth was, I was already enough.

Under the leadership of my counselor, I began to address the roots of these issues. I began to journal, pray, and allow myself to ask and be asked the hard questions. I was

DEEPER Women™ Teach

willing to be accountable to the knowledge that came from the answers to these hard questions. Once you know better, you do better, right? The most authentic, unapologetic, and unadulterated version of you is where freedom resides. Our feelings are there for a reason -- not to be pushed aside or asunder. Looking back, I now see that to me, they were there as a checkpoint. Feelings are your body's internal check engine light. So, I challenge you - the next time you begin to feel anxious, worried, sad, and nervous; or the like, ask yourself WHY DO I FEEL LIKE THIS? Address it, assign it so you can move through it, and become intentional about the way that you're living your life.

Allow me to address this very quickly as well - our favorite hood rat duos, fear, and doubt, will crop its ashy-ankled, corn chip smelling self- up. I would like to share a quick story. A girlfriend suggested that I start a podcast and I was like "Uh no... how in the world am I going to do that?" My first instinct was to address and validate the fear that

DEEPER Women™ Teach

instantly rose within me. Then doubt, who did not trail her musty self too far behind quickly chimed, "Yeah!" Who wants to listen to you? What makes you the benchmark for success? You live in an apartment! You ain't got no higher degree. Did you write a book or something that we don't know about?" *insert a praise report here because here I am, you know, writing a book! *

* Back to our regularly scheduled programming *

What are you saying Jamia? What I am saying is, do not be surprised if those thoughts arise as you are walking on the path to healing. Give yourself grace and change the tape. Take out the "Woe it's You" side A and pop side B in— the "Woah, it's You!" on repeat friend.

I am learning about the power to choose using the CTFAR Model - Circumstance, Thoughts, Feelings, Actions and Results. It walks through how our thoughts affect our feelings. The circumstance may not change but our thoughts and feelings around it CAN. I have learned that I must make a choice every day; one that will serve me mentally and emotionally even if and especially when there are circumstances beyond my control.

Do not get me wrong, I could most certainly complain! I mean, our housing situation is less than ideal, par-ent-ing is HARD, COVID, family, money, interviews, debt repayment (thank you med school), jobs, extracurricular activities, health and only God knows, WHERE WILL WE GO NEXT?!?! I mean, it is enough to stress about, believe you me. Every day, we must make a choice. We must choose the thoughts that serve us mentally and emotionally.

It is important that you speak against every negative thought and emotion that would seek to deter or block you from moving forward. Start asking yourself better questions. Start requiring better of yourself - not more - but better. Use each opportunity as a chance to do things a little differently. Be kind to yourself. The things you have been carrying are heavy so laying it down will feel strange, but I beg of you; do not pick them up again. Leave them there. Hand back the things that do not belong to you back to their original owner. You are not a trauma repository. Start slow but for heavens' sake, start.

It is important that you institute some boundaries and apply them across the board. Boundaries will need to be set at work, home, in your marriage, with your family and your children. At the end of a long day I used to say, "Mom's done!" meaning if your head is not rolling down the hall separate from your body and the house is not on fire, do not come find me. Be prepared to pass out some grace to your family as well - it is new for them too. Take heart! This is not impossible! In fact, it is reversible. My counselor always says, 'You cannot talk your way out of situations you behaved your way into." It is going to take some work and a whole lot of action!

DEEPER Women™ Teach

It is important that you teach others how to treat you by modeling it...and here is the kicker, modeling it in love. Respect is a way of treating or thinking about something or someone with a deep admiration. So, start with yourself. Respect yourself enough to say, no this is not how I want or deserve to be loved and I will not accept it. We are done tying worthiness to productivity. Without having done one single thing, you are worthy of the love you need and deserve.

It is imperative that you discover your identity beyond just who you are to others or what your business card lists as your occupation.

Yes, it can absolutely be scary to feel like you have bared your soul to the world. In this new season, we must become comfortable discovering our hearts and relearning ourselves. Only then can we answer with confidence when we are asked the question, "who are you?" It's ok to not fit inside someone else's box, but we must own and accept who we are so we grow into living our best life.

DEEPER Women™ Teach

Find that thing that is burning within you. Reignite your passion and get back to whatever gets you to some place of centered-ness. Do not tell me you do not have the time. Make it. We are moving from breakdown to breakthrough. Pain = progress. Do not forfeit, friends. I promise you that neglecting you will not fulfill your family. You figure it out for everyone else. This time do it for yourself.

You see, just a year ago, I had no clue who I was. Today, I stand proudly and proclaim that I am the creator of **The Mrs. Beside** of which I am MOST PROUD! I am no longer afraid. I am happy. I am whole. I am courageous. I am brave. I have no lack. I am chosen. I am called to encourage. I am equipped by God to fulfill my purpose on this Earth. I am confident. I am walking in my purpose. I am loved. I am exactly where I am supposed to be. I am fearfully and wonderfully made. I am NOT forgotten. I am influential. I am intelligent. I am perfectly imperfect. I am a forgiver and forgiven. I am more than my past mistakes. I am more than

DEEPER Women™ Teach

the trauma I've experienced. I am NOT a failure. I am exactly the Mother that my children need. I am the wife that my husband desires. I am living a life of faith. I am in a place of abundance. I am gifted. I am peaceful. I am calm. I am passionate. I have the favor of God. I am healthy. I am successful. I am grateful. I am empathetic. I am compassionate. I am trustworthy. I am responsible. I am unique and **I AM MORE THAN ENOUGH**! I AM MORE THAN THE MRS.

Who Are You?

By Dr. Marcea Whitaker

DEEPER Women™ Teach

There is that moment in life when we ask ourselves this important question "Who Am I?" It usually comes after…after the kids have left for college, after we have ended that relationship, or maybe after we have left the cemetery. It could also occur after that natural disaster or after we have left our office cubicle for the last time.

It is in the AFTER that many people find themselves alone and without purpose. The air is still but the sound of nothingness is deafening. It is in the after where there is a knowing that there should be something there, but there is nothing. Our heartbeat seems to pound in our heads. Our stomach feels uneasy as if we are about to throw up; but there is nothing there. We are empty.

I recall this question of "Who am I?" coming up when I was leaving a 19-year marriage which had been laden with emotional abuse. My cup was empty. I had no more fight. I was living below my potential and I knew it; but I could not move. I had tried to leave, and I had tried to stay. I had the fear of the unknown.

Why had I stayed so long? It could have been fear of the unknown. Where would I go? What would I do? How would I pay my bills? It could have been fear I would be out of the will of God if I left. Was I supposed to stay and just wait for the promise that it would get better? Throughout this time, I did not recognize me. Where had I gone? When did it happen? Who was I anyway? How do I now find me? Do I backtrack and get the old version? Where do I look? I could not even determine when I lost it. All I knew was that I did not know who I was. Who was I anyway? What did I stand for? I did not know. What if I could not find me?

In the end, I chose to look for the answers. I chose to lean in. I chose to embrace this challenge—this journey—and not run away from it. My journey started by investing in myself to become a life coach. What I discovered can help you find you.

DEEPER Women™ Teach
#1 You Get to Create Your Own Experience.

Are you living in a reactionary mode? …Someone did X, now do you do Y? Do you wake up wondering what is going to pop off or what is going to go wrong? When obstacles do come, do you wonder what you did to cause them; or do you take it as a sign you were not supposed to go in that direction?

I used to live this way. I would be afraid of challenges and thought of them as bringing me harm. I would believe they were a sign that I had made the wrong decision either back then or just right now; or I used to believe that it was God showing me that I was going in the wrong direction. Does this sound familiar?

I am an Internal Medicine physician. I remember deciding I wanted to be a doctor while still in middle school. My best friend and I both had the same idea. We decided independent of each other that we were going to both become pediatricians and open a medical office together. I remember counting the investment- four years of college, four years of medical school, three years of residency, and how much money it would cost. I also thought about whom I could help. I started crossing off the list where each would lead me to my goal, one at a time. Let me tell you, there were MANY obstacles! Test after test. There were one-hour tests, four-hour tests, and eight-hour tests. Some tests took me six months of preparation. The greatest tests occurred when there was a living and breathing person on the other side of the stethoscope and I was charged with deciding the medical plan for them, which could easily mean life or death.

Did I ever FEEL like quitting? Yes, yes, and YES; but did I ever think this path was not for me because of the obstacles? NO.

Twenty-seven years later now, I have saved some, healed some, and touched some. While I did not end up becoming a pediatrician and joining my friend (who ended up becoming a pediatrician), I did become an Internal Medicine

DEEPER Women™ Teach

physician - a doctor for adults. Along the way, I stepped into my purpose of leading women to a different type of internal medicine. It was and is leading them to a place of internal peace; to a place where they know things do not happen to them, but for them. It is leading them to a place where they do not allow the things that happen define who they are, to a place where they get to decide what their own experience looks like to a place where they get to control what they can control and learn to accept whatever happens next.

The takeaway is that you get to create your own experience. So, what do you want your life to look like? What do you have control of?

#2 You Get to Decide... *and then you get to decide how you want to think about your decision.*

Whose brain are you using to make your decisions? I was trapped. I had boxed myself in. I was a shell of a person. Sure, I looked like I was fine. I was dressed and present and accounted for. My kids made it to all their events, school, play dates, and practices. They always had what they needed- meals, clothing, a place to live, and much, much more; but I was only going through the motions. I was EMPTY.

I realized I was gifted with different talents and if I did not know how to do something, I was confident I could find out by the time tomorrow. With that came lots of ideas, some great and the rest mostly good, with a rare bad idea sprinkled in. However, because of what was expected of me as a wife, how I was made to feel and how emotionally empty I was, I dimmed my light. I dummied down. I lived below my potential. I started anticipating what decision would be made and then pulled back or re-adjusted what I said or did to "make it better," to "not make waves," to comply with the program". I, in essence, put up additional walls INSIDE the box I was already trapped in.

I remember being asked where I wanted to go to eat. Immediately, I would start thinking where other people would want to eat and then try to make a choice that I thought would be amenable to everyone. Worse yet, I did not even know where I wanted to go. It was the moment of apathy. I just wanted someone else to make the decision. I just wanted to get it over with. What a sad place when you do not even know what you want or remember you have a choice. I look back now, and I see the pain and how it has affected me.

In essence, I was using someone else's brain, someone else's thoughts, someone else's desires to make all MY decisions. How crazy is that? Listen, it is ok to have an opinion, to have a desire, to have a say, and to say it OUT LOUD! Many of the women I work with need to give themselves permission: permission to think, permission to have an opinion, permission to just say it. Wow, what liberation! What freedom!

How do you get to this place?

Decide. Decide what you want and what you do not want. Decide it is ok if it does not line up or is contrary to what others around you think. Here is the key. I am not saying it is your way or the highway. It is not all about you. It is fine to compromise. I am saying that you can know what YOU want initially and then go from there. Imagine finding a great find at a flea market. Negotiation only happens after the seller gives you a price and then you SAY that you are willing to pay the price. NAME YOUR PRICE! Stop being afraid to say it. Stop accepting only what others give you. The only thing you can be sure of is if you do not say it, (or you are waiting for someone to read your mind), you will not get it.

What happens AFTER you say the thing? I am glad you asked. You then get to decide how you think about the decision you just made. We all get to that place where we have made the hard decision and now the next day we are now living with the decision. Maybe, others have criticized the decision. You start second-guessing yourself. You start regretting what you did or said. Panic sets in. Fear of what will happen next comes upon you. You start to retreat.

Let me help you out of that place. You have stepped out of your comfort zone and your body, mainly your brain, does not like it. There is a part of your brain that is charged with keeping you safe. Whether it is seeking to be safe from the grizzly bear, that is chasing you or from that bad relationship or the soul-sucking job you must have because it is paying your bills, this part of your brain HATES change, ANY change.

In this powerful moment, you get to decide how you think about the decision you made. Ask yourself; is that how you really feel? Did you make the original decision because it was in line with what you wanted and what you were feeling at the time? If the answer is yes to both, then you just decided that you agree with the decision you made. Now, you can move on to the next step (i.e., the next paragraph). If the answer to either is no, additional work is needed.

DEEPER Women™ Teach

For many decisions, the morning-after decision is where the fight happens. You will have to keep making THAT decision repeatedly until you can overpower that part of your brain.

#3 Validation is for Parking

There are two types of people. There are people who place more value on what others think about them and people who place more value in what they think about themselves. Which one are you? I believe there are more of us that fall into the first category. I was one. I have not been able to figure out why this is. Is it the nature of our society? Is it an innate or genetic trait? Is it a learned behavior that we need to be intentional about? Regardless of the why, I believe we have the power to alter it.

When we are more concerned with what others think, feel, or say, we end up right back in that box. Trapped. We become dependent on others' approval, second guessing most of our moves, spending our days, months and years being held hostage by the need to stay in our comfort zone. I have this birthmark on my face. Because of how I THOUGHT people thought about it, it affected how I showed up in the world. I thought it was ugly and it shaped how I viewed myself. It affected what I did or did not do where I went, and what I decided to do. I did not look people in the eye. I did not stand up for myself when I could have or should have. I spent ten years of my early life trying to get over it. Ten years were lost until I decided that I loved me no matter what others thought. How I thought became most important.

Here is a sobering reality. People do not really care that much about you as much as you think they do. They are more concerned with themselves. Think about the news cycle. The average time for a typical big news story is one week. If you think about it, that is just one week for a news story to reach its peak and then fizzle out before it becomes yesterday's news. One week! No matter how big. You change your life or make big decisions that you then must live with for the rest of your life for *one week*. Seeking external validation from someone who will not even remember that it mattered to you is something that needs to be considered seriously.

One of my favorite affirmations or beliefs is "Validation is for parking and not for people." Your thoughts and actions do not need to be co-signed by those around you. Family, spouse, co-workers, strangers, bosses, even children do not need to affirm what you think or what you choose to do. What could you accomplish if you did not waste time thinking and overthinking your moves? How much extra time would you save? What else could you accomplish? Other people do not have the right or authority to live your life for you. Decide that internal validation is more important than what anybody else thinks.

Who do you want to be? It is time to move. It is time to move from what you have been doing to who you want to be.

DEEPER Women™ Teach

Nobody Knew the Journey
By Nile Yates

DEEPER Women™ Teach

On October 31, 2019, I was diagnosed with Stage 1 Breast Cancer. At that time, there were many things going on with my family—a lot of moving parts. So, I kept the diagnosis a secret from my family and friends for three months. I thought that if I shared, people would perceive me as weak or think my life was less than perfect.

I had spent most of my life worried about what others thought of me; trying to be the best at everything—at home and at work; the best wife, the best mom, the best daughter, niece, friend, and…the best leader.

I was at the office when I received a call. *Mrs. Yates…You're going to have to have another mammogram and an ultrasound."* Immediately following the appointment, I was told that I would have to have a biopsy. I am sitting in my office (again) the following week when I received another call. This time I am told that I need to see a breast surgeon for a complete diagnosis. I stay strong while on the phone. I am detached and unemotional. I take copious notes. I am hearing everything and writing it down. I am holding back my tears. I am still in my office at work. Everyone has gone home for the day, at least I think. Then one of my employees walks into my office. I am crying, but I cannot tell her what is wrong. I am still in shock and in disbelief. I tell her I am okay. I tell her that something just made me sad, but I am okay, really, I say. I wipe my tears as fast as I can and begin sipping on my water. She leaves. The next day, the same employee drops off a bag of my favorite goodies to spread sunshine into my day. I thank her and yet I still cannot open my mouth to share my devastating news – my newfound information.

In comes another employee who begins talking to me about his health struggles and fears. I am holding on to his every word. What he does not know is that I have been given a complete scare from my doctors. I stay strong for the employee. I listen intently without saying a word. While I am listening, I want to scream, but I cannot. I have been told so many times to be strong. I cannot cry now because I do not want to have to explain my tears. I cannot cry now because I do not have any answers to my WHY. I cannot cry now because I am at a new job, and I cannot show my emotional side. So, I hold back my tears and focus on the person talking. He is discussing his cancer diagnosis and the treatment plan. I begin blocking my fears and anxiety and dig deeper into supporting this person. At the same time, I am reflecting on how open he is about his fears and anxiety. I listen in amazement because I am fascinated by his strength despite his concerns. I sit there nodding my head. I say *I understand*. I am comforting myself at the same time I am comforting him.

Often, as leaders we make other people a priority. We focus on helping everyone, but sometimes we lose focus on helping ourselves. As a servant leader, we have been taught to take the "I" out of our vocabulary. It is not about YOU. It is about your students, staff, and community. Since I have been conditioned to focus on others, it is easy for me to push my feelings to the side and block what is really happening in my life at this very moment. It is called channeling your inner strength; even when you sometimes do not even know your inner strength has that much power.

Let Yourself Break

The blinds were closed throughout the house. The kids were at school. The house was eerily quiet. I had been lying in bed all day. I had not eaten anything. I do not even know if I got up to use the restroom. What I do remember is, asking Cory to leave the house when he came to check on me the third or fifth time. "Cory please leave the house. I need to be alone. I want to tear up some stuff, I want to fight someone, I want to let my feelings out and destroy the house. Cory, I cannot do it while you are here. I am trying to be strong, but I am about to break." *I am not leaving. Hit me, do what you need, I am not going anywhere.* Within seconds, I began hitting, screaming, and punching. When I finished breaking, my man was right there holding me and would not let me go. What he would say to me next, I use to carry me even on my strong days—*Baby, I got you. I am built for this…and so are you.*

I Am Not My Hair

As the oncologist is talking, my husband and my mom are both present. I do not hear a single word after "I am putting you on a treatment plan"; except two simple words—hair loss.

Everyone knows at least one of the major side effects of chemotherapy is hair loss. As the doctor was telling me all the side effects of chemotherapy, the one I did not want to hear about was hair loss. The one side effect I was not ready to grasp was hair loss. Why? This would make the devastation of having this terrible disease a reality for me. Losing my hair would make the cancer real. I could not hide from the breast cancer diagnosis. I could not pretend it was not me. Everyone would know. That was the last thing I wanted. I did not want my natural state to change. If I changed physically, then that would open the speculation and judgement from people and it would be something so real. I would have to face it head on. So, as the doctor opened his mouth and the words I did not want to hear were uttered, I ran out of his office. I ran to the nearest elevator.

If I could have laid out on the floor, I would have, but Cory…Cory was there and literally held me up. I just could not wrap my mind around having to go through chemo. When I heard I was going to have to have chemotherapy with accompanying hair loss, I was completely gut punched. If I were a betting woman, and you had bet me 10 million dollars, I would have my hair shaven. I would have laughed in your face and said HELL NO!

Two weeks later, I asked my husband to completely shave my head. I sat in the kitchen with a towel over my shoulders. I cried, but I knew it was what needed to happen. So, I sat there. I accepted what needed to happen.

DEEPER Women™ Teach

I Had to Get Help

My wake-up call was the day Cory called my doctor on my behalf concerned about my well-being. The doctor referred me to a therapist and all I needed to do was make the appointment. Let me say I was angry then too! I was mad at myself for not being strong enough to get through the situation, not being strong enough to hide my emotions, and that I was not using my faith. Usually, I will cry one good cry and then I put on my "fake it till you make it" composure and get through life. But this time the wind was completely knocked out of me and I fell flat on my butt. Yes, I was angry that I had to make the appointment, but grateful that Cory knew I needed additional support. At my first appointment with the therapist, all I did was literally cry and cry and cry. She gave me a couple of apps to listen to during the first visit. I signed up for my next appointment.

She gave me more suggestions to help me cope. My third appointment was a teleconference due to COVID-19 and during this meeting; I cried a little less and laughed a little bit more. This time, she gave me more strategies to cope-one of my favorites was the one she gave me to get ready for my treatments. Treatments made me sad. She suggested that I turn the radio on and listen to some hardcore rap. *You can listen to gospel music the next day, but treatment days is all about the DIVA in you.* When she said that I quickly related and then was in awe that she saw the DIVA in me. So, as angry as I was that Cory felt like I needed to see a therapist, I went because I knew he was right. I now have a standing appointment. It has been immensely helpful going to see a therapist while going through breast cancer and just to handle everyday life. Did you know there are therapists who just work with patients of breast cancer? My therapist is a therapist for just breast cancer patients, which is neat because she totally gets the crazy things that come out of my mouth.

We cannot choose the music that life plays for us, but we can choose how we dance to it. – Author Unknown

DEEPER Women™ Teach

Put on Your Lipstick and Act as If

I am tired. I can barely get out of the bed. When you are depressed and going through chemotherapy, the simplest things are the hardest things to do. I took for granted getting dressed, bathing myself, walking to the master bathroom or going up a flight of stairs. Until you just do not have the energy in you, you will not realize how much effort this can take. I did not have the energy. I was tired. I was sad. Yet, every morning I rolled…I mean literally rolled out of bed, because I had no upper body strength. I slowly walked to the bathroom. I put on clothes; chose my jewelry of the day, and grabbed a matching head wrap…Wait! Do not forget the eyeliner, mascara, and lipstick! Where am I going when I am dressed and all made up?—the next room…the sofa; because by now, I need a nap.

My children would laugh at me daily. They would ask, "Where are you going? My hope was if I looked good, I would feel good. Yet there were days when I went for treatment and all I wanted to do was wear some sweatpants and a hoodie. However, I did not. I got dressed as if I was going to work. My mom would always tell me sometimes all you have is your personality and your appearance. Sometimes it is not about the college degrees and all the letters behind your name. It is about how you are nice to others and how you are presenting your best self. So, throughout this journey putting on my lipstick was more than just trying to be cute. It honestly was about surviving and trying to find hope. When you are feeling hopeless: get dressed; comb your hair, put on your lipstick, and walk as if the world owes you something. Walk in confidence even when it's fake. It will give you an ounce of strength and the ability to push through.

You Will Always Need Your Mother

My mom, stayed with us in Georgia for three months after my initial surgery. She took care of the house and our teenage children. My mom traveled to Georgia for all my initial appointments from her home in Texas. I remember the day I called my mom from the parking garage of the hospital before I went in for my mammogram with Cory. I called her but the words did not come out, just sobs. I wanted my mom, but I had not yet told her what was going on. I did not want to worry her, but at that moment, I needed to hear her voice. I needed her to pray. I needed her to go to my late dad's favorite chair and pray. I needed her to say it is going to be okay. Yes, my mom prayed. I prayed. Cory prayed. Though God did not answer my exact prayers, He made no mistake. The road I traveled with the diagnosis could have been worse, but it was detected early, and it gave me a different perspective on life. My mom loves to say – You can keep ripping and running, but God will sit you on your behind. Listen to the wisdom of your parents.

DEEPER Women™ Teach

The Lesson

Cancer did not care about what others thought or how I felt about what people would say. Cancer came to teach me who I was and why I am here. Clearly, I had failed to see the big picture. Who really cares about other people's comments? I realized later that the bigger picture was to tell the story of how Breast Cancer was God's way of preparing my family and me for our next promotion in Life.

Meet the Authors

OF

DEEPER Women™ Teach!

DEEPER Women™ Teach

Dr. Barbara Swinney

In a period of six months, I got a divorce, accepted a reassignment from one leadership position to another at work, bought a house, sold a house, sent a child off to college, and started a life and leadership coaching business to help women in leadership transition through life changing events. …All of this in the middle of experiencing the roller coaster ride of my own healing process, and fastening the seat belts of my two daughters as they navigated their new reality. Nobody could help me. I trusted no one to give me the grace that I needed should my performance fall below the level of excellence to

DEEPER Women™ Teach

which I had become accustomed. So I suffered in silence…I powered through.

This is not just my story. This is the story of many women in leadership. Instead of having a place to process our personal problems, we stuff them; we put on our Ruby Woo lipstick, our finest suits, and stylish heels, paint a smile on our faces…and we walk—confidently insecure—bound by the expectations of others, paralyzed by self-judgement, and completely afraid to give any indication that we're not OK.

This…is my why! This is why I became vigilant about helping women, like me, transition through life changing events, while managing the demands of their roles as leaders; this is why I wrote the books, "It's Always DEEPER" and "Leading the DEEPER Way". This is why I hosted the DEEPER Women™ Speak —an event that provides a platform for women in leadership to share their after their

DEEPER Women™ Teach

dreams, to lead the DEEPER Life, and become DEEPER Women™!

I am Dr. Barbara Swinney, leader of more than 25 years, a John Maxwell Certified Life and Holistic Leadership Coach and Coach Trainer, Speaker, Author, Founder and CEO of the DEEPER Leader Institute for Personal and Professional Development; using my gifts to inspire transformational thinking and being to help leaders clarify their vision and align their personal, professional, and organizational goals so that they are able to serve their purpose and the broader community from any position.

CONNECT WITH DR. SWINNEY:

- barbaraswinneyinc.com
- barbaraswinneyspeaks.com
- info@barbaraswinneyspeaks.com
- info@thedeeperleaderinstitute.org
- FB, IG, Twitter: @bswinneyinc
- LinkedIn: Dr. Barbara Swinney

DEEPER Women™ Teach

OTHER TITLES BY DR. BARBARA SWINNEY

Available

Amazon and barbaraswinneyinc.com

DEEPER Women™ Teach

Dr. Leona Allen

Dr. Leona Allen is the founder of Freedom Health Systems which is dedicated to helping women achieve more *FREEDOM* in their health and their life!

Dr. Leona is known for her innovative programs that help busy, professional women transform their health and their life, by removing the physical, chemical and emotional barriers to natural healing.

For many years, Dr. Leona lived with chronic headaches, fatigue, and weight gain, only to find out that it was due to pre-diabetes and fatty liver disease. Understanding the serious impact this could have on her life, she became determined to discover what it would take to heal her body. Her journey to healing has been a major turning point in her health, her life, and the way she runs her practice.

Programs developed by Dr. Leona are customized based upon a thorough health assessment. She believes that a person's current health status is a reflection of the stressors the body has endured over an extended period. Dr. Leona works closely with her patients to develop plans designed to reduce the negative effects of physical and emotional trauma, nutritional deficiencies, chronic cellular inflammation, and toxicity.

Dr. Leona received her Bachelor of Science degree in mechanical engineering from Michigan State University, and her Doctorate of Chiropractic degree from Life University. As a licensed Chiropractor, of almost 20 years, Dr. Allen's practice has evolved to embrace more of a whole body, natural health care approach.

Dr. Leona is the proud mother of two energetic boys, has a 1st degree black belt in Taekwondo, and is active in CrossFit. She also enjoys traveling, dancing, and cuddling up with a good book.

To learn more about how you can get to the root cause of your health problem and begin to rebuild your body at the cellular level, visit DrLeona.com.

CONNECT WITH DR. LEONA ALLEN:

DRLEONASPEAKS.COM	INSTAGRAM	@DR.LEONA
HELLO@DRLEONA.COM	FACEBOOK	@DRLEONA
	LINKEDIN	@DRLEONA
	YOUTUBE	@DRLEONAALLEN
	TWITTER	@DRLEONAALLEN
	PINTEREST	@DRLEONAALLEN

DEEPER Women™ Teach

OTHER TITLES BY DR. LEONA ALLEN

Available on Amazon

DEEPER Women™ Teach

Pamela Dingle

It sounds so cliché, *Broken to be Blessed*, but these are the exact words that define my story. I once saw an intriguing photo of a grove of trees with wide, solid bases that stood resolute, planted and strong yet their limbs had been bent and leaned towards a light or source of energy seeming disconnected from the location of their trunks. This photo so aptly created an image of the experience that I seek to describe here to share with you the insights I gained and how God used this moment in life to move me on to my purpose.

DEEPER Women™ Teach

I was born in Indianapolis, Indiana on March 19, 1963. A turbulent time in history as courageous leaders sought to change how I would experience my life and journey through the transformation of the rights of all people in the United States as promised by our ancestors, yet our nation had failed to execute in fact. Initially unaware of the turmoil around me in which this transformation was seeded and foddered, I grew and developed within.

DEEPER Women™ Teach

Jeri Godhigh

Jeri Godhigh is a driven leader in the Acworth, Georgia community, a dynamic public speaker and life-changing coach. She leads by example and real life experiences in her coaching. Godhigh is exhilarating, humorous and engages her audience with charisma and passion. Godhigh is the founder and real estate broker of the Godhigh & Associates Realty Company that she started in 2017. Before the inception of her company, Godhigh has led a successful real estate career for the past 16 years. Godhigh is naturally talented in the art of real estate sales and leads over one million in revenue. Godhigh desires to help millennials through the home buying experience and help to make it an excellent experience. She has built a solid foundation of corporate clients and relocation throughout her 16-year tenure in the industry. She is a current real estate instructor with the American Real Estate University where she teaches the fundamentals of sales.

Godhigh is also the CEO, Agency Owner of the Godhigh Agency Allstate Insurance Company in Kennesaw, Georgia where she leads a seasoned sales team. She and her team are invested in being trusted advisors to families, individuals and executives in their local community. She has built an impressive financial portfolio consisting of life, auto, retirement and home insurance within a short period. Insurance sales falls right in Godhigh's wheelhouse of skills, she enjoys consulting and educating the community on their options in insurance and in the home buying process.

Godhigh has been recognized for her work and was featured in *Formidable Magazine* as one of the "Queens of

DEEPER Women™ Teach

Real Estate" in the Atlanta Metropolitan area. She has also been featured in the American Lifestyle Magazine showcasing real estate articles. She is a minister and the chaplain of the Love Jones Foundation and has served as a district and local leader for the Georgia PTSA. In her downtime Godhigh loves spending time with her family and friends. She has been married for 30 years to her husband Robert Godhigh and they have four wonderful children and six beloved grandchildren.

This year Godhigh partners with her daughter, Jamia Ponder, to bring you *Jeri & Jamia: Unfiltered,* a powerful and necessary movement, created to help mothers & daughters heal and break generational curses. Both women are certified life coaches who help mothers and daughters make strides to heal completely. "Unfiltered" has launched a podcast aimed to heal a nation of mothers and daughters and help break generational curses often carried over in silence. Godhigh and Ponder also offer the "Unfiltered" coaching program, designed to help coach mothers and daughters to a healthy space, to release past hurts, grudges, and pain. In addition, they intend to launch an annual "Unfiltered" Brunch designed to celebrate and bridge mother and daughter relationships.

DEEPER Women™ Teach

Lorarine Loving

Educator, motivator, preacher, mother, and certified professional coach: Lorarine Loving is a native of Greenville, Mississippi. She is known for her tenacity and her fighting spirit.

Life has taught her that plans change, and the journey can be downright tumultuous. After being jilted and left to raise a daughter by herself, she found herself wondering through life with no direction. She met someone whom she felt like was her forever love. They were married and had a daughter. But this marriage proved to be a dark period in her life. Once again, she found herself alone and now with two daughters with a big age difference (almost fifteen years). On top of this, her finances were a mess and she filed bankruptcy several times. She also gained a lot of weight and became very sluggish. Fast forward to 2019, she went for her routine mammogram and was diagnosed with Stage 0 breast cancer. Yes, in the infamous words of Langston Hughes, life for her had not been a "crystal stair."

Through it all, she has learned to F.I.G.H.T. for herself and her daughters. Every day she fights to change her self-destructive habits and negative mindset. She is finding her way by entering what she calls the *"No Excuse Zone"* and learning to **F**orgive, **I**ntentionally Live, **G**et Moving, **H**aving Hope, and not getting **T**ired.

Lorarine is an Itinerant Elder in the African Methodist Episcopal (AME) Church. She is an associate minister at St. Andrew AME Church in Memphis, Tennessee where she serves on the women's ministry leadership team, as the leader of the financial literacy ministry, as the Dave Ramsey's

DEEPER Women™ Teach

Financial Peace University coordinator, and as the social media coordinator. She earned a Bachelor of Arts in Elementary Education from Tougaloo College and a Master of Education in Curriculum and Supervision from Delta State University. She became a certified professional coach in 2018 after attending Atiras International Coaching Academy. After being a classroom teacher in Mississippi and Tennessee in rural, suburban, and urban areas for 23 years, Lorarine now serves the state of Mississippi as a literacy coach. She is a proud member of Alpha Kappa Alpha Sorority, Incorporated.

Lorarine lives in Olive Branch, Mississippi with her mother and her two daughters (Jean-Imani and Jolanna). She is appreciating her singleness while waiting to meet her future husband. She enjoys traveling, learning interesting and weird facts, reading, cooking, and spending time with her family.

DEEPER Women™ Teach

CONNECT WITH LORARINE LOVING

LorarineLoving@gmail.com

https://www.facebook.com/CoachLorarine

https://unapologeticpraise.wordpress.com/.

DEEPER Women™ Teach

JAMIA PONDER

Jamia Ponder is the Founder and Creator of The Mrs. Beside—a movement and safe space dedicated to celebrating women, wives and mothers standing BESIDE and NEVER behind their spouse. From full time jobs, last minute dry cleaning, kid pick up, drop off, grocery shopping, planning, bills, budgeting, chauffeuring, cooking, exercising, eating (somewhat) right, play dates and an expected chandelier swing from time to time, SHE KNOWS WHAT IT TAKES…And whew girl, I S S A L O T! As a Mom of three and the wife of a Medical Physician, she has been there every

DEEPER Women™ Teach

step of the way! She spent years and years behind the shadows, supporting her husband through Medical School working numerous jobs just to put food on the table. Mom'ing. Budgeting. Volunteering. Encouraging. Pushing. Walking BESIDE and oftentimes in front of her husband. Making preparations that had yet to cross his mind. Taking care of things that never crossed his path. Effortlessly. Patiently. Silently…And seemingly, unseen. So, when Graduation Day arrived, she was over the moon thrilled! He graduated! He did it! Yet simultaneously she felt an indescribable pang; and it was the pain of lack. Four years of carrying it all with seemingly nothing to show for it. So, she sought some help and her counselor asked, "Jamia, what are you most proud of? Not your kids. Not your hubby. But YOU." It was in that pivotal moment that she realized it was time to add herself BACK on her To-Do list! She is more than the MRS. and you are too!

DEEPER Women™ Teach

DR. MARCEA WHITAKER

Dr. Marcea B. Whitaker is a Board-Certified Internal Medicine Physician, Life Coach, Dynamic Speaker and Author, and has been featured in Columbia Inspired Magazine. Dr. Marcea's journey lead her to become the coach she always needed and she is now the CEO of In Full Bloom Health and Life Coaching where she helps professional women break out of their personal prison of life and finally live life without limits. She is also the Founder of Women Ready to Move Academy, where she equips women to Discover themselves, Decide what they want and get to their Destination.

DEEPER Women™ Teach

Dr. Marcea is well-qualified and is proud to have attended an Historically Black College/University (HBCU). She received a Bachelor's of Science from the University of Maryland Eastern Shore graduating sum cum laude, before earning her medical degree from West Virginia University. She has practiced medicine for over 25 years and appreciates the role the mind plays in wellness. She has also served in public health for almost 2 decades. Her other accomplishments include member of Phi Kappa Phi Honor Society, Business of Medicine Certificate from Johns Hopkins University, Women's Ministry Leader and Member of Alpha Kappa Alpha Sorority, Inc.

Dr. Marcea is the mother of two teenagers and enjoys daily exercise, laughter, and deep conversation. She embraces new experiences as a way to step out of her comfort zone and she sees challenges as only opportunities.

DEEPER Women™ Teach

CONNECT WITH DR. MARCEA WHITAKER:

Website: www.InFullBloomHealthandLifeCoaching.com

Speaker Website: www.DrMarceaBSpeaks.com

FB: https://www.facebook.com/infullbloomhlc/

IG: @marceawhitaker

LinkedIN: : http://linkedin.com/in/LifeCoachMarcea

DEEPER Women™ Teach

NILE YATES

Wife, Mom, Educational Leader, Mentor/Coach

Nile Yates, the proud daughter of accomplished public-school administrators, is also a public-school leader with a 'student first' philosophy. Nile believes that if school leaders grow and develop teachers, the teachers will grow and develop the students, and we will see substantial growth in the school communities.

Mrs. Yates' educational career journey began as a Sunday School Teacher and Mathematics Tutor. She went on to earn a Master's Degree in Educational Leadership from Texas

DEEPER Women™ Teach

A&M University-Commerce. Mrs. Yates began her professional career serving as a Third Grade Teacher and was later promoted to Dean of Instruction and Summer School Principal at a Title 1 school. In 2005, Nile relocated to Marietta, Georgia and served as a Seventh Grade Teacher, before being promoted to Assistant Principal.

Mrs. Yates' tenure in both Texas and Georgia, has given her the unique opportunity to work and lead diverse campuses, ranging from low to high socioeconomic schools. This experience has shaped her belief that all students can achieve academic excellence with collective care and intentional instruction. She believes that, "no matter the zip or area code, students want to know that you care, parents want the best for their children, and faculty and staff want a servant leader."

As an administrator, Mrs. Yates was recognized by district leadership for being instrumental in the school receiving 'Recognized' status for the first time in the school's history. As a part of the leadership team, schools where Mrs. Yates has served, have been recognized by the United States Department of Education for school-wide excellence in promoting health, wellness, and environmental education, earning the National Green Ribbon School Distinction award. Additionally, one of the schools was recognized by the state of Georgia for successfully implementing a school wide Positive Behavior Intervention and Support program that led to the school receiving a personal 'Distinguished' honor from the Georgia State Superintendent. Mrs. Yates continues to achieve astonishing results, supporting a high socioeconomic school, achieving Districtwide STEAM Certification and recognition as a National Blue-Ribbon School.

In her spare time, Mrs. Yates supports others by coaching and mentoring aspiring administrators through college preparatory programs. Under Mrs. Yates' tutelage, six teachers and mentees have been promoted, including four new Assistant Principals. Mrs. Nile Bolden Yates is a member of Alpha Kappa Alpha Sorority, Incorporated. She married her college sweetheart. Together they have two children.

DEEPER Women™ Teach

www.ingramcontent.com/pod-product-compliance
Lightning Source LLC
Chambersburg PA
CBHW031146160426
43193CB00008B/268